WHITE SUPREMACY

DARK LEGACY

ALLEN POLLENS

Allen Pollens

ISBN-13: **978-1542778374**
ISBN-10:**1542778379**

DISCLAIMER

Any resemblance to individuals, corporations, and places is mostly coincidental. Exceptions to this are well-known cities and other locations presented with a reasonable amount of legitimacy to maintain realism. Other exceptions included are well-known events which as much as possible are attributed as far as the sources.

Allen Pollens

DEDICATION

I dedicate this book to the memory of all of the victims of hate crimes in this country (USA) and elsewhere around the globe.

Allen Pollens

CONTENTS

Allen Pollens

ACKNOWLEDGEMENTS

Writing a book of this magnitude is a colossal undertaking and I must first, and foremost acknowledge my dear friend Robert who never fails to encourage me, assist in any required research and provides the very first assessment of the story as it develops chapter by chapter. Thank you, Robert.

Allen Pollens

PREFACE

Authenticity has always been important to me in what I write. I allow myself reasonable liberties within the context of fiction. In this case, the subject is so upsetting that I have wondered long if I should write this story at all. However, I have lived more than three-quarters of a century and have personally witnessed much that has taken place… was even personally substantially affected by what took place during World War II. I was 12 years old at the end of the war when full accounts of the Holocaust became known.

In 1905 my father and his family made their way out of Russia to immigrate to this country. My mother's family immigrated here also in 1905 from Romania. My father was in his late teens. My mother was yet to be born. All Jews.

My father never denigrated his life in Russia and, on the contrary, told pleasant stories of his growing up. My father's stories were so lacking a negative tone that, finally, I asked him, "Then why did you leave?" His response included a word I had never heard before. "The pogroms," he answered.

Although we were exceptionally non-observant, I knew I was a Jew. Revelations of the Holocaust indelibly marked me. I felt that "I had to be a Jew." To be less would have meant turning my back on six million people who the Nazis killed because they were Jews. Ironically were it not for the immigration of my father and his family; I might have been a concentration camp victim sent to the gas chamber.

Allen Pollens

PROLOG

My name is Joy, and my role is central to this story. By its very nature, this is a difficult tale, and I'm writing this Prolog without knowing what the outcome will be. However, you need to know that the subject material has to deal with the growth in racist hate and hate of Jews and a few other hatreds as well. Where did it all start, at least in a big way? Adolph Hitler and the hatred that coalesced around him was at the core of it. I'm sad to say that he may be gone, but what he started, lives on in today's' world. I am pleased to share my story with you up to the writing of this Prolog. I'm 61 years old, as of time if this telling, and have had a good life. No one can take that away from me no matter what. Read on, and in the end, we'll both know how it all turns out.

Please note that preponderance of Nazi/Nazism information presented in this book is real, not fiction!

We Should All Be As One, Joy Levinson

Allen Pollens

Chapter 1 – The Encounter

Sunday, October 2, 2016, Local Residential Street on the Outskirts of the City of Portland Oregon

Joy, Joyce Levinson was on her way home from food shopping at a supermarket nearby her home

. Joy didn't have far to go but had misjudged the number of bags and the weight of it all. She stopped several times and struggled to readjust the load. She was near to giving up and to calling someone on her cell phone to help her. Then, a voice behind her said, "Let me help you with your bags."

Joy turned. She recognized a young man she had noticed in the area, several times.

"I would greatly appreciate it," she responded. "You must be from here. I remember seeing you around. I'm Joyce Levinson by the way, and you are?"

"I'm Eddie, Eddie Rawlins."

"Well, Eddie Rawlins, you are saving the day for me. You sure, you want to do this? I was just about to call someone, and was thinking who the person might be."

"Not necessary. Let's divide up these bags, and be off to your house."

They were under way, in short order. Joy thought, *What a nice young man.* Breaking the silence, she offered, "My place is just a little way down the street. It's one of the attached ones, not quite as private as I would like but it is spacious and comfortable. There it is. The beige and blue one in the middle of the complex."

"Looks nice," responded Eddie, while thinking, *Joy, I already knew exactly where you live.*

Eddie followed Joy into the house and the kitchen.

"Putting my shopping away will take a few minutes, Eddie," Joy advised. "May I make you lunch? I have some excellent looking roast beef that I just bought. I could make you a sandwich with all the fixings along with coffee or a Coke."

"Nice… yes, I would like that," responded Eddie even as he wondered, *Why is this Jew bitch being so nice to me? No doubt is preparing me for something else that she wants. I hope Frederic will give me the go ahead soon to bring this to an end.* A little insecure, he reached around under his hoodie, and his shirt to where he kept his gun inside his pants and under his belt. *Whew, still there, good!*

"You look a little out of sorts. Are you OK? Still want a sandwich?" Joy queried.

"Yes," he nodded, forcing a smile. Then thought, *It better not be on Jewish Rye!* "What kind of bread?"

"Oh," answered Joy, "nothing special, your choice," she began.

Oh boy, here it comes, he thought.

"Just regular white or whole wheat," advised Joy

Eddie continued in a high state of stress, never for an instant forgetting Joy was to be his first Jew victim. He knew he was to proceed with this as part of a Frederic coordinated action. He was the man. Frederic was also the father figure who replaced the one that failed him in so badly.

"Regular or wheat," Joy repeated, "and how about a slice of provolone cheese on top of the roast beef? I'll warm it enough in my toaster oven to start the cheese beginning to melt."

"Yum," Eddie answered and meant it. He marveled at how deftly Joy proceeded.

Then, in almost no time at all, she placed the sandwich, with potato salad and dilled pickle down in front of him.

"Joy, is it a **kosher** dill?" he asked.

"Hmm," she pondered and then went into the small pantry. "No," she continued. "It's a good brand not identified as kosher. Try it out. You'll like it anyway."

Relieved, Eddie took a bite of the pickle and while munching it, gave thumbs up. "Very good," he added, as he went at the sandwich.

Joy watched as he attacked the meal in an almost ravenous fashion. "It's nice to have someone here to prepare a meal for."

Still chewing his food, Eddie mumbled, "You going to eat? Are you married?"

Joy laughed..."I had eaten before I went shopping and I live alone, not married. It's a lonely existence, my friend, but I'm grateful for the wonderful years I had with John."

"John?" puzzled Eddie, between mouthfuls of food.

"My husband, John Levinson. He was killed last year in an unfortunate accident."

John Levinson, the Jew, Eddie silently considered. *That leaves me to deal with just you.* "You're Jewish," Eddie blurted.

"Only the name…Levinson," Joy responded.

"Yes, but you were born Jews, and, whatever your plans were for the future, you were still Jewish.".

"The seriousness of the accusation caused Joy to go quiet until Eddie was near finishing off his meal. The *Still Jewish*" suggestion deserved a well-considered response. "Let's move over to the living room," she, requested, "I'll get to the dishes a little later."

On entering the living room, Joy said, "I'll sit over here on my favorite cushy armchair, and you can make yourself comfortable on the couch. Also, why don't you take off your hoodie?"
Eddie nodded and proceeded to take it off.

As he removed it, Joy saw an upsetting emblem. "Gees!" She yelled. "There's a swastika on your back!"

"OK, OK," Eddie tried to calm her. I forgot about it."

"You forgot about it? Forgot about it? How could you forget about it?"

"It's on the backs of my shirts, and I don't see it myself," Eddie tried to explain.

"Is it tattooed on your body as well?" she pressed, breathing heavily.

"No, not yet," Eddie answered honestly.

"You're with one of those hate groups that are after hurting and killing Jews and blacks and everyone else that doesn't measure up to white standards, aren't you? Am I a possible target because I'm thought to be a Jew? Am I your target?"

"I, uh I, uh," Eddie stammered.

"DO YOU HAVE A GUN, A GUN ON YOU RIGHT, NOW? DO YOU?" Joy shouted even as she started to cry.

Eddie started to get up to try to calm her somehow.

"DON'T!" Joy yelled out, "Just sit there until I figure this out."

After a while, Joy more calmly said, "I need to get something to drink. I want you to come into the kitchen and sit with me at the table, across from me at the table."

Eddie silently nodded his agreement. Joy beckoned him to get up and go ahead of her. She followed.

In the kitchen, Joy made herself a cup of French Vanilla coffee out of her K-Cup brewer and then waited for Eddie to pick out something and do the same.

Joy sat looking across the table directly into Eddie's downcast face. Finally, she said, "I want you to tell me everything."

"Everything?" Eddie pondered aloud.

"Everything, my friend," she responded sarcastically. I want to know your whole life's story from the earliest time that you can remember right up until this minute. I want to know who you are!"

"But, that could take a long time." Eddie protested.

"Oh, you have a hot date, or need to meet with the swastika, boss? Let it out, and I'll consider what we should do or… maybe I'll just call the police. The police? Yes? Or your life story before I take a step with that, you may not like. Let me be straight with you. I'm 61 years old, and I can either throw you to the wolves who are waiting out there to eat you up or help you to find a better way to live your life. It's your choice, the wolves or me.

"BULLSHIT! I'm getting out of here right now, and you can't stop me! I'm sick and tired of being told what I can or cannot do. You sound like my fucking father never satisfied with anything about me. Now, I decide what to do!"

"Do you?" pressed Joy. "What about your swastika club? What's the name of your contact? In what ways do you have to answer to him? Or her? How about this whole Levinson name thing and being Jewish? Are you supposed to kill me, when they tell you it's time?"

Eddie couldn't believe what Joy was saying. Frederic told him when the time was right; it would be easy. *Maybe I shouldn't have tried to know more in advance by taking advantage of the chance to help her with her bags. Pa always said I never knew the right*

10

thing to do. "I got to go, got to get out of here!" he
pleaded.

Realizing the extent of his upset, Joyce said, "Let us
reset," Then she pressed him back into his seat and
handed him a handful of tissues.

"I never get anything right," Eddie murmured, as an
avalanche of tears burst forth, his face still buried in his
hands.

Joy waited a considerable time. Then she asked,
"Have you so far done anything to hurt anyone?"

"No," came the muffled answer. "No," Eddie
repeated.

"Good," responded Joy and she waited a significant
time in silence.

Finally, Eddie sat up and looked around. "I better go
now," he said.

"Go where?" Joy softly asked.

"I don't know… maybe Frederic."

"Is he your main contact in the swastika place?" queried Joy

"Yes," answered Eddie in a subdued way.

"How much do you know. Eddie, about the history of all this?" Joy probed.

"You mean Hitler and all?"

"Yes."

"Not much. Frederic promised to fill me in when we have more time."

"I will make a bargain with you Eddie," offered Joy. "If you will tell me more about yourself, I will help you to know all about Adolf Hitler and his legacy to the present day."

"Won't that take a lot of time, maybe more than a day?"

"Do you have something special to do or someplace you must go?"

Eddie shook his head, no.

"Where do you go at night, where do you sleep?"

"Where ever I can. It's not always the same place."

"Are you a street person?"

"I… I… am," he admitted.

"Here's my deal, take it or leave it. If you want to leave, I won't stop you as long as you promise not to come back another time to hurt me. Also, you would have to promise to turn yourself into the police before you would hurt anyone else. I couldn't live with myself if I let you go and you hurt another person."

Eddie breathed deeply and then nodded his head. He followed with, "How will all this work?"

"While we are doing this, you can stay with me in the guest room I have, but you would have to agree to put your gun under lock and key."

"Joyce, why are you willing to do all this?"

"Maybe it's because of John, and me never having any children together. We probably should have adopted, but didn't. Also, I like you. I think you have it in you to be a good person with special abilities not yet discovered."

Eddie was clearly touched. No one had ever expressed anything like this to him before. He held back more tears and asked simply, "Where do we begin?"

I have a small safe installed in my bedroom where we will secure your gun. I'll return it to you when we finish if you still want it and you promise not to hurt anyone with it. The best thing would be for you to get rid of it altogether, but I'm getting ahead of much we need to accomplish.

"Okay, I'm ready," Eddie said with just a hint of a smile on his face

Allen Pollens

Chapter 2 – Eddie's Story & Hitler I

Sunday, October 2, 2016, Home of Joyce Levinson, Near 6:00 PM

"Eddie, what do you think of the accommodations?" asked Joyce as he was coming out the guest room.

"They're very nice. Thank you. What do we do now?"

"You relax or watch the news on the TV in the living room while I pull together some dinner."

"May I help you?" Eddie wanted to know.

"Maybe with clean up. I have everything well under way."

"May I sit at the table here in the kitchen... maybe chat with you.?"

"Okay, but be aware that if you engage me in too much conversation, it may delay dinner. Only kidding, Joy chuckled. "Here's a glass of sangria. I'll get you something if you don't care for wine."

"I like sangria."

"Sip away. There's plenty more, within reason. Turn on the radio over on the counter, or if you're up to it, check a news station to see what's up in the Trump-Clinton race for the Presidency. Have you been following it?"

"No, I just know that Frederic is leaning toward Trump," shared Eddie.

"Well, it'll all be over soon and, here for tonight, ta da, is my famous pasta primavera courtesy of Ragu and some others. To go along with it here is some Parmigiano Reggiano to sprinkle on top. Try it out and let me know what you think."

Eddie sprinkled the parmesan, wound pasta on his fork which he then carefully put in his mouth. "Hmm," he managed, and then his eyes opened wide. "WOW, this is delicious. I can't remember the last time I had a meal like this," lauded Eddie.

"Well, it's the last meal for the condemned man before telling his life story."

"Hmm, what a way to go!" Eddie responded.

Joyce didn't say anything but was pleased with the good humor, ahead of the more serious discussion she was planning after dinner.

By 7:30 PM, they were finished with dinner and in the living room with Joy ensconced in her favorite armchair and with Eddie seated comfortably on the couch.

"Where shall I begin?" started Eddie.

"How about with your age, Eddie?"

"I turned 22 on my last birthday, in May."

"Did you finish high school?"

"Tenth grade. I couldn't stand the home situation anymore and couldn't keep going to school after being out on my own."

"Do you have any siblings?"

"A sister but she's almost ten years younger'en me."

"What about your mother and father?"

"My mom is a good woman but has had a hard life. She was seventeen when I was born, out of wedlock. My

16

father married her but didn't love her. He took off when I was two years old, and I don't remember anything about him."

"Grandparents?"

"They're out in Michigan someplace, Detroit I think. My mom finally ran away to Oregon because of me being born out of wedlock and my father deserting her. Being here alone was hard, but she was still a good looking woman. She met Morris. He was smitten enough to marry her but always treated me like I was necessary unwanted baggage. Never played ball with me or did the other things dads did with their kids."

"How," asked Joyce, "did that make you feel?"

"Worthless and as much as my mother tried to compensate, I blamed myself for not being good at anything. When I was sixteen, I had enough of Morris's put downs. I whacked him on the head with a frying-pan, knocked him out, and left never to return."

"That's awful. How have you managed to get by?"

"Catch as can. Work, usually temporary, when I can get it. Sometimes I steal or pick pockets and handbags. Nobody wants to invest in someone like me. And then, I look around and see black guys and Mexicanos taking away good jobs from guys like me, while Jews are raking in all the money.."

"And how does Frederic fit into all this?"

"He knows what a white person should have and that there should be places, maybe a bunch of states set aside for whites, only and no Jews. Says Hitler was right, and we should appreciate his legacy."

"Do you go along with all this?" asked Joy.

"I do, and Frederic says the more I know, the more I'll realize what must happen. Says I'm smarter than most people realize and am a dependable soldier."

"Eddie, I have experienced much over the years that I can share with you. It allows me a perspective of how all this, Nazism, Neo-Nazism, Skinhead, and White Supremacy got started and what is going on today." Shall I tell you about all I have learned over the years? Do you want to take this journey with me?"

"Will you be angry with me if I still want to be with Frederic?"

"I have confidence in the person I think you are and along the way, I am going to help you to reach into yourself and know at your core who you are and what your strengths are."

"I'm not sure about everything you're talking about, especially the last part. Do you still want to do this with me? I may not be worth the time."

"I suggest you tell Frederic that you have some personal matters to attend to and will not be available for a while. Will you do that?"

"May I have my gun back?"

"I'll consider it if and when you return from your meeting with Frederic."

"Okay, I'll try to find him in the morning. May I go to bed now?"

"Of course, but you have to be up by eight if you want some breakfast before you set out. I'll be looking forward to your return and our journey into the past."

"Good night, Joyce."

"Sleep well, Eddie."

Monday, October 3, 2016, Home of Joyce Levinson, Near 8:00 AM

Joy was cooking something on the stove when Eddie entered the kitchen. He seated himself at the table which was already set out for two. Glancing over her shoulder, she greeted, "Morning, Eddie. Did you sleep well?"

"I did, Joyce. Thank you."

"Ready to talk with Frederic about not being around for few days, that is if you still want to go through with what we talked about yesterday?"

"Yes, Joyce," he responded while considering, *I may still have to kill you. Frederic expects it when the time is right.*

"Okay my friend," Joyce said as she placed a plate of scrambled eggs, pan fried potatoes, and bacon strips in front of him, "have at it. Want some coffee or orange juice?"

"Coffee with milk and sugar, please." *I have to hold her off at arm's length... remember Frederic says she's a Jew bitch even if she denies it.*

Eddie enjoyed the food as much as he could considering his inner turmoil.

Monday, Oct. 3, 2016, Feistys Office Location, 10:30 AM

Eddie stood in front of the door for a long time contemplating what he would tell Frederic.

He was surprised when the door suddenly opened.

"Eddie!" Frederic exclaimed.

Eddie immediately took note of the young man standing next to Frederic who he did not know.

"This is our newest recruit, Frank," Frederic advised.

"Good morning, Eddie," offered Frank. "I'm leaving. Perhaps we can get together for a chat another time."

"I'd like that," Eddie responded, unsure, still feeling off-kilter about meeting with Frederic.

Frank edged past Eddie and Frederic stepped forward to welcome Eddie with his usual warm hug. "Well, this is a nice surprise," he said as he escorted Eddie inside. "What's up? Take the seat next to my desk, and we'll talk. I'm free until 1:30 and we can do lunch together." Frederic waited for Eddie to respond.

"Y-yes, lunch is good. I walked by Pizza-Spezziel on my way here. Is that what you have in mind?"

"Yes, Eddie, but Spezzi, Spuzzi, Schmutzi, the main thing is your update on what's happening with the Jew Levinson. Under control?" queried Frederic.

"Yes," responded Eddie with faked confidence.

"You know," reminded Frederic, "the Jew pigs are practiced at self-benefiting deceit. Have you seen this?"

"Oh, yes," Eddie responded strongly. He was relieved when Frederic did not question him on specifics.

Frederic raved about the importance of their mission and how Jews had gotten away with selfish activities. "They should never have been allowed to steal Palestine from the rightful Arabic residents. We have no choice but to fight them in every way, everywhere." Frederic railed on and on until at near the end of the lunch. He

21

then turned his attention to Eddie's circumstances. "Talk to me about Joyce Levinson, Eddie," he requested

"She knows how I feel about Jews. Lies Levinson may be a Jewish name but that she has never been a Jew. Wants to tell me she knows about Nazism... the main reason I came by today. If I am to humor her until our plan is ready, I will not be available for a while."

"You're on the front-line, Eddie. Can you handle this?" Frederic wanted to know.

"Of course," Eddie responded strongly to hide doubts that Joyce was raising.

They ended lunch with Frederic congratulating Eddie on his efforts and telling him to stay the course,

Monday, Oct. 3, 2016, Home of Joyce Levinson, 2:00 PM

Eddie waited for Joyce to come to the front door.

"Hi Eddie," she said. "Everything cool with Frederic?"

"He's knee deep with other stuff, and I think he's happy to be free of spending the time with me right now," he partially lied.

"Good, let's go into the living room and get started."

They took their accustomed seats, Joyce in the cushy armchair and Eddie sitting on the couch.

"Do you have a preference where to begin? It's okay if you don't because I think I know the best place."

"Tell me, please, Joy, err, Joyce."

"You can call me Joy, and I'll call you Ed or Edward if you prefer."

"I'm Eddie to everyone."

"So be it, Eddie. Now to where we can begin? It may surprise you, but I know a lot about how the whole Nazi thing began and, to simplify our discussions, I will use the designation 'Nazi' as often to refer, to these as well: Neo-Nazi, Skinhead, White Supremacist, and so on. As I said, I know a lot about how all this began. Since I'm 61, that means I was born in 1955, and you may ask yourself, 'How can Joy know so much?' True?"

Eddie nodded his agreement.

"It was from my father," Joy revealed.

Eddie was intrigued but also jealous of the relationship he never personally had.

"When I was ten years old, I told him I wanted to know more about World War II, and he told me everything from the very beginning, including about his time in the military. So we, start with Adolph, Adolph Hitler. I have two printed copies of information that I found online at Wikipedia. We can take turns reading and discuss it afterward. Shall I start, Eddie?"

Eddie nodded, and Joyce began:

Hitler was born in Austria, then part of Austria-Hungary, and raised near Linz. He moved to Germany in 1913 and was decorated during his service in the German Army in World War I. He joined the German Workers' Party, the precursor of the NSDAP, in 1919 and became the leader of the NSDAP in 1921.

"NSDAP," interjected Joyce, "is defined in a later reading as the 'Nationalsozialistische Deutsche Arbeiterpartei' (NSDAP)," She continued reading.

In 1923, he attempted a coup in Munich to seize power. The failed coup resulted in Hitler's imprisonment, during which time he dictated the first volume of his autobiography and political manifesto Mein Kampf ("My Struggle"). After his release in 1924, Hitler gained popular support by attacking the Treaty of Versailles and promoting Pan-Germanism, anti-Semitism, and anti-communism with charismatic oratory and Nazi propaganda. Hitler frequently denounced international capitalism and communism as being part of a Jewish conspiracy.

By 1933, the Nazi Party was the largest elected party in the German Reichstag, which led to Hitler's appointment as Chancellor on 30 January 1933. Following fresh elections won by his coalition, the Reichstag passed the Enabling Act, which began the process of transforming the Weimar Republic into Nazi Germany, a one-party dictatorship based on the totalitarian and autocratic ideology of National Socialism. Hitler aimed to eliminate Jews from Germany and establish a New Order to counter what he saw as the injustice of the post-World War I international order dominated by Britain and France. His first six years in power resulted in rapid economic recovery from the Great Depression, the effective abandonment of restrictions imposed on Germany after World War I, and the annexation of territories that were home to millions of ethnic Germans—actions which gave him significant popular support.

Adolf Hitler, From Wikipedia, the free encyclopedia

Adolph Hitler in 1938

Hitler sought Lebensraum ("living space") for the German people. His aggressive foreign policy is considered to be the primary cause of the outbreak of World War II in Europe. He directed large-scale rearmament, and on 1 September 1939 invaded Poland, resulting in British and French declarations of war on Germany. In June 1941, Hitler ordered an invasion of the Soviet Union. By the end of 1941 German forces and the European Axis Powers occupied most of Europe and North Africa. Failure to defeat the Soviets and the entry of the United States into the war forced Germany onto the defensive, and it suffered a series of escalating defeats. In the final days of the war, during the Battle of Berlin in 1945, Hitler married his long-time lover, Eva Braun. On 30 April 1945, less than two days later, the two killed themselves to avoid capture by the Red Army, and their corpses burned.

Under Hitler's leadership and racially motivated ideology, the Nazi regime was responsible for the genocide of at least 5.5 million Jews and millions of other victims whom he and his followers deemed Untermenschen ("sub-humans") and socially undesirable. Hitler and the Nazi regime were also responsible for the killing of an estimated 19.3 million civilians and prisoners of war. Also, 29 million soldiers and civilians died as a result of military action in the European Theatre of World War II. The number of civilians killed during the Second World War was unprecedented in warfare and constitutes the deadliest conflict in human history.

"What do you think about any or all of this so far, Eddie?"

"I think it doesn't end here."

"I agree with that but let's discuss this whole significant happening before we move on. Let's go back and just look at the first paragraph first and Hitler's writing of 'Mein Kampf.' Do you realize what he was advocating and who he was blaming?"

"I guess that's the way he saw it.

"Doesn't the fact that he attempted a coup in Munich in 1923 tell us anything?"

"That he didn't care for the existing government?"

"Or, maybe he was hungry for power? Let's table this for a while, but was not *Mein Kampf* part of a continued effort to gain power?"

"Are we going to table it or not?"

"I'm sorry, Eddie, let's move on. However, the article advises Hitler was on the move after his release from prison in 1924 and found his voice in blaming much of everything bad on a Jewish Conspiracy.

"But look at the success he had by 1933, Joyce, Hitler's appointment as Chancellor."

"Yes the first step in '*transforming the Weimar Republic into Nazi Germany, a one-party dictatorship based on the totalitarian and autocratic ideology of National Socialism.*'"

"Yes, and maybe the best thing for the German people!" underscored Eddie.

"We're far from over with this," responded Joyce, "but what is the best thing for Americans and who classifies as such anyway?"

"Whites but not Jews."

"Really? Do you realize we are essentially a nation of immigrants? If not us directly, then our parents, or grandparents, or great-grandparents or..."

"Yeah, just let every riff raff in the door."

"Settle down Eddie we have a long way to go before we can finish off with this. Let's cut to the last paragraph which summarizes Hitler accomplishments:"

- Genocide of 5.5 million Jews and millions of other victims,
- Killing an estimated 19.3 million civilians,
- 29 million soldiers and civilians dead, due to military action,
- A war classed as the deadliest conflict in human history.

"Maybe... maybe it was necessary," Eddie said quietly.

"Millions and millions of people killed? I think you are a better person than that, Eddie. Let's put all this away and move toward some dinner."

"Does that mean we're over battling with one another for tonight?"

Joyce pondered for a bit and then shifted gears. She growled and put on the most menacing look she could manage. "No, grr, I'm after cooking up something. You can try to call out Frederic's whites or Nazis, but they'll be facing an army of hook-nosed Jews, grr. Let' go out to eat."

"You're crazy."

"Yeah but to know me is, is..."

"Crazy."

"Sanity starts at 9:00 AM tomorrow and, by the way, we have only just scratched the surface on Adolph Hitler. What he fomented and the legacy he left is far too significant to leave without delving more deeply into all of it. I also want to share with you, my father's recollections of how everything here in the United States changed almost overnight during World War II."

Allen Pollens

Chapter 3 – Hitler II

Tuesday, October 4, 2016, Home of Joyce Levinson, 9:00 AM

"You did say we were getting started at nine o'clock this morning," Eddie wanted to confirm as he entered the kitchen.

"Right on, my friend. I needed to identify and print out a guide for our talk this morning. Your copy is right there on the table near to where you seated yourself yesterday."

Eddie sat down, picked up the print out and read the title at the top of the document:

Adolph Hitler Information Excerpted From Biography.com.

Quickly surveying it, his eyes opened wide as he noted the five major categories:

- Early Years
- Rise to Power
- World War II
- Legacy
- Japan in WWII

"Are we going into <u>all</u> of this, Joy?" Eddie questioned.

"Yes, before people go around hurting or killing one another, they should know all of the facts. Don't you?"

"Well I do, but I thought that it was the job of people at the top to figure that out. You know, ahead of recruiting others to do what they need to do. Oh, yum," he blurted as Joy put a repeat of the prior day's breakfast in front of him."

"So Frederic is the guy who has to have figured it out or maybe the person above him."

"Is that not the way it has to work?"

"We're off on a tangent here, and I want us to focus more directly on the subject at hand, Hitler. Let me ask you to remind me later about Lyndon Johnson, the Vietnam War, and 50,000 Americans killed in that debacle."

With a puzzled look on his face, Eddie said "You'll need to explain to me about 'tangents' and 'debacles.'"

"Just enjoy breakfast before we better know Hitler," Joy said as she set down her eggs, potatoes, and bacon.

They then moved to their usual living room places and took turns reading from e Biography.com document aloud:

Early Life

Dictator, Adolf Hitler was born in Braunau am Inn, Austria, on April 20, 1889, and was the fourth of six children born to Alois Hitler and Klara Polzl. As a child, Hitler frequently clashed with his father. Following the death of his younger brother, Edmund, in 1900, he became detached and introverted. His father did not approve of his interest in fine art rather than business. In addition to art, Hitler showed an early interest in

German nationalism, rejecting the authority of Austria-Hungary. This nationalism would become the motivating force of Hitler's life.

Alois died suddenly in 1903. Two years later, Adolf's mother allowed her son to drop out of school. After her death in December 1907, he moved to Vienna and worked as a casual laborer and a watercolor painter. Hitler applied to the Academy of Fine Arts twice and rejected both times. Out of money, he moved into a homeless shelter, where he remained for several years. Hitler later pointed to these years as the time when he first cultivated his anti-Semitism, though there is some debate about this account.

"Not impressive," observed Joyce. "You think?"

"No, it's not," Eddie reluctantly admitted, "but I can identify with some of Adolph's troubles."

"I guess you can, Eddie, but would he be blaming Jews for lack of another source of his difficulties?"

"Maybe, let's read on to see where this all goes, Joyce," Eddie eagerly pressed.

"Yeah."

In 1913, Hitler moved to Munich. At the outbreak of World War I, Hitler applied to serve in the German army. He was accepted in August 1914, though he was still an Austrian citizen. Although he spent much of his time away from the front lines, Hitler was present at some significant battles and wounded at the Somme. He was decorated for bravery, received the Iron Cross First Class and Black Wound Badge.

"He sure looks different in the first picture," a surprised, Eddie commented.

"Definitely," Joy agreed. "I'll continue reading..."

Hitler became embittered over the collapse of the war effort. The experience reinforced his passionate German patriotism, and he was shocked by Germany's surrender in 1918. Like other German nationalists, he believed that the German army was betrayed by civilian leaders and Marxists. He found the Treaty of Versailles degrading, particularly the demilitarization of the Rhineland and the stipulation that Germany accept responsibility for starting the war.

After World War I, Hitler returned to Munich and continued to work for the military as an intelligence officer. While monitoring the activities of the German Workers' Party (DAP), Hitler adopted many of the anti-Semitic, nationalist and anti-Marxist ideas of DAP founder Anton Drexler. Drexler invited Hitler to join the DAP, which he did in 1919.

"Thus," breaking away from her reading, Joy said, "we have the source of Hitler's hatred of Jews."

"As well," added Eddie, "as his anti-Marxist feelings and nationalist fervor."

"It added up to Hitler needing someone to blame, you think, Eddie?" asked Joy.

"I don't know if I agree with that," he replied with a frown.

Joyce decided Eddie was still committed to Frederic and company and decided not to respond. She instead went on with the reading.

To increase its appeal, the DAP changed its name to the Nationalsozialistische Deutsche Arbeiterpartei (NSDAP). Hitler personally designed the party banner, featuring a swastika in a white circle on a red background. Hitler soon gained notoriety for his vitriolic speeches against the Treaty of Versailles, rival politicians, Marxists, and Jews. In 1921, Hitler replaced Drexler as NSDAP party chairman.

"As I suggested earlier, he needed someone to blame, Eddie," Joy stated.

"Maybe he had some good reasons we do not know about," he said in a more determined way.

"Right," responded Joy, sarcastically, "I don't think so. Scapegoating can be very useful. Let's continue."

Hitler's vitriolic beer-hall speeches began attracting regular audiences. Early followers included Army Captain Ernst Rohm, the head of the Nazi paramilitary organization, the Sturmabteilung (SA), which protected meetings and frequently attacked political opponents.

On November 8, 1923, Hitler and the SA stormed a public meeting of 3,000 people at a large beer hall in Munich. Hitler announced that the national revolution had begun and declared the formation of a new government. After a short struggle including 20 deaths, the coup, known as the "Beer Hall Putsch," failed.

Hitler was arrested three days later and tried for high treason. He served a year in prison, during which time he dictated most of the first volume of Mein Kampf ("My Struggle") to his deputy, Rudolf Hess. The book laid out Hitler's plans for transforming German society into one based on race.

"What a nice guy?" Joyce couldn't resist.
"No comment," Eddie responded, unwilling to agree.

Rise to Power

The Great Depression in Germany provided a political opportunity for Hitler. Germans were ambivalent to the parliamentary republic and increasingly open to extremist options. In 1932, Hitler ran against Paul von Hindenburg for the presidency. Hitler came in second in both rounds of the election, garnering more than 35 percent of the vote in the final election. The election established Hitler as a strong force in German politics. Hindenburg reluctantly agreed to appoint Hitler as chancellor to promote political balance.

"What a mistake that was," Joy commented.
"Hindenburg obviously felt he had no choice," Eddie responded confidently.
Joyce decided not to challenge Eddie about it at this point. She continued reading.

Hitler used his position as chancellor to form a de facto legal dictatorship. The Reichstag Fire Decree announced after a suspicious fire at the Reichstag, suspended basic rights and allowed detention without trial. Hitler also engineered the passage of the Enabling Act, which gave his cabinet full legislative powers for four years and allowed deviations from the constitution. With full control over the legislative and executive branches of government, Hitler, and his political allies embarked on a systematic suppression of the remaining political opposition. By the end of June, the other parties had been intimidated into disbanding. On July 14, 1933, Hitler's Nazi Party was the only legal, political party in Germany.

"Goodbye freedoms but people are sometimes like sheep," said Joy.

Eddie, with pinched eyebrows, asked, "Why? Because they didn't feel this was a bad thing?"

"Yes, and politicians know how to maneuver sheep. Joy motioned to Eddie to pick up on the reading."

The military opposition was punished. The demands of the SA for more political and military power led to the Night of the Long Knives, which took place from June 30 to July 2, 1934. Ernst Röhm and other SA leaders, along with some of Hitler's political enemies, were rounded up and shot.

"Well isn't that a nice way to resolve some differences?" Joy felt necessary to say. "This ugliness continues as part of Hitler's legacy today. Watch out for Frederic. No one is safe around people with these kinds of muddled reasoning. No, that is not the worst of it because it only comes down to a question of, 'What's good for me?' or what is good for my movement? Eddie, to get along with them, you must serve them and not question the validity of the beliefs they promote."

"Frederic is not like that, Joyce," Eddie advised adamantly.

"Right, let us continue. We have much more to cover." Joy began reading further.

The day before Hindenburg's death in August 1934, the cabinet had enacted a law abolishing the office of president and combining its powers with those of the chancellor. Hitler thus became head of state as well as head of government and named formally as leader and chancellor. As head of state, Hitler became the supreme commander of the armed forces. He began to mobilize for war. Germany withdrew from the League of Nations, and Hitler announced a massive expansion of Germany's armed forces.

"WOW!" exclaimed Joyce. "All of this accomplished by the man who applied to the Academy of Fine Arts twice and rejected both times. Then, out of money, moved into a homeless shelter, where he remained for several years."

Eddie looked displeased with her assessment and countered, "I think he deserved a commendation for what he overcame."

Eddie, Eddie, thought Joyce, *I hope I can show you the light.* Joy continued reading.

The Nazi regime also included social reform measures. Hitler promoted anti-smoking campaigns across the country. These campaigns stemmed from Hitler's self-imposed dietary restrictions, which included abstinence

from alcohol and meat. At dinners, Hitler sometimes told graphic stories about the slaughter of animals in an effort to shame his fellow diners. He encouraged all Germans to keep their bodies pure of any intoxicating or unclean substance.
A main Nazi concept was the notion of racial hygiene. New laws banned marriage between non-Jewish and Jewish Germans, and deprived "non-Aryans" of the benefits of German citizenship. Hitler's early eugenic policies targeted children with physical and developmental disabilities, and later authorized a euthanasia program for disabled adults.

The Holocaust was also conducted under the auspices of racial hygiene. Between 1939 and 1945, Nazis and their collaborators were responsible for the deaths of 11 million to 14 million people, including about 6 million Jews, representing two-thirds of the Jewish population in Europe. Deaths took place in concentration and extermination camps and through mass executions. Other persecuted groups included Poles, communists, homosexuals, Jehovah's Witnesses and trade unionists, among others. Hitler probably never visited the concentration camps and did not speak publicly about the killings.

Joyce decided, as hard as it would be not to comment on the horrors leading up to and during World War II, she would remain silent. Perhaps it would be the best way for Eddie to digest it all.

World War II

In 1938, Hitler, along with several other European leaders, signed the Munich Agreement. The treaty ceded the Sudetenland districts to Germany, reversing part of the World War I Versailles Peace Treaty. As a result of the summit, Hitler was named Time magazine's Man of the Year for 1938. This diplomatic win only whetted his appetite for a renewed German dominance. On September 1, Germany invaded Poland. In response, Britain and France declared war on Germany.

Hitler escalated his activities in 1940, invading Norway, Denmark, France, Luxembourg, the Netherlands, and Belgium. Hitler ordered bombing raids on the United Kingdom, with the goal of invasion. Germany's formal alliance with Japan and Italy, known collectively as the Axis powers, was signed to deter the United States from supporting and protecting the British.

On June 22, 1941, Hitler violated a non-aggression pact with Joseph Stalin, sending 3 million German troops into the Soviet Union. The invading force had seized a huge area before the German advance was stopped outside Moscow in December 1941.

On December 7, Japan attacked Pearl Harbor in Hawaii. Hitler was now at war against a coalition that included the world's largest empire (Britain), the world's greatest financial power (the U.S.) and the world's largest army (the Soviet Union).

Facing these odds, Hitler's military judgment became increasingly erratic. Germany's military and economic position deteriorated along with Hitler's health. Germany and the Axis could not sustain Hitler's aggressive and expansive war. In late 1942, German forces failed to seize the Suez Canal. The German army also suffered defeats at the Battle of Stalingrad and the Battle of Kursk. On June 6, 1944, the Western Allied armies landed in northern France. As a result of these significant setbacks, many German officers concluded that defeat was inevitable and that Hitler's denial would result in the destruction of the country.

"And they were correct," emphasized, Joyce.

"Okay," responded Eddie unwilling to discuss it. Frederic's influence remained strong.

"Continue with next section, Eddie," urged Joyce.

Death and Legacy

By early 1945, Hitler realized that Germany was going to lose the war. The Soviets had driven the German army back into Western Europe, and the Allies were advancing into Germany. On April 29, 1945, Hitler married his girlfriend, Eva Braun, in a small civil ceremony in his Berlin bunker. Around this time, Hitler learned of the assassination of Italian dictator Benito Mussolini. Afraid of falling into the hands of enemy troops, Hitler and Braun committed suicide the day after their wedding, on April 30, 1945. Their bodies ended up in the bombed-out garden behind the Reich Chancellery, and burned. Berlin fell on May 2, 1945. Five days later, on May 7, 1945, Germany surrendered unconditionally to the Allies.

Hitler's political program had brought about a world war, leaving behind a devastated and impoverished

Eastern and Central Europe, including Germany. His policies inflicted human suffering on an unprecedented scale and resulted in the death of an estimated 40 million people, including about 27 million in the Soviet Union. Hitler's defeat marked the end of a phase of European history dominated by Germany and the defeat of fascism. A new ideological global conflict, the Cold War, emerged in the aftermath of World War II.

When Eddie finished reading, Joyce advised, "I have been bothered by the shortness of Biography.com's treatment of Hitler's legacy and reviewed some of the other sources. I found this that I printed out from Wikipedia." She proceeded to hand out a copy to Eddie. "Let's go over it now, but you'll note as we get into this, a difference in the total estimate of deaths caused," she said.

"Is it more than 40 million?" asked Eddie.

"Closer to 50 million," advised Joyce. "Either way it is staggering. I'll start reading from the new handout, and we can talk more about the total killed later if you wish."

Hitler's suicide was likened by contemporaries to a "spell" being broken. Public support for Hitler had collapsed by the time of his death, and few Germans mourned his passing; Kershaw argues that most civilians and military personnel were too busy adjusting to the collapse of the country or fleeing from the fighting to take any interest. According to historian John Toland, National Socialism "burst like a bubble" without its leader.

Hitler's actions and Nazi ideology are almost universally regarded as gravely immoral; according to Sir Ian Kershaw, "Never in history has such ruination—physical and moral—been associated with the name of one man." Hitler's political programme brought about a world war, leaving behind a devastated and impoverished Eastern and Central Europe. Germany itself suffered wholesale destruction, characterised as Stunde Null (Zero Hour). Hitler's policies inflicted human suffering on an unprecedented scale; according to R.J. Rummel, the Nazi regime was responsible for the democidal killing of an estimated 19.3 million civilians and prisoners of war. In addition, 29 million soldiers and civilians died as a result of military action in the European Theatre of World War II. The number of civilians killed during the Second World War was unprecedented in the history of warfare. Historians, philosophers, and politicians often use the word "evil" to describe the Nazi regime. Many European countries have criminalized both the promotion of Nazism and Holocaust denial.

"And yet," commented Joyce, "we have all kinds of organizations, including Frederic's, today based on Nazism."

Unsmiling, Eddie shrugged, not willing to argue with her.

"Please read the last paragraph, Eddie," Joyce requested.

Historian Friedrich Meinecke described Hitler as "one of the great examples of the singular and incalculable power of personality in historical life." English historian Hugh Trevor-Roper saw him as "among the 'terrible simplifiers' of history, the most systematic, the most historical, the most philosophical, and yet the coarsest, cruelest, least magnanimous conqueror the world has ever known." For the historian John M. Roberts, Hitler's defeat marked the end of a phase of European history dominated by Germany. In its place emerged the Cold War, a global confrontation between the Western Bloc, dominated by the United States and other NATO nations, and the Eastern Bloc, dominated by the Soviet Union. Historian Sebastian Haffner avers that without Hitler and the displacement of the Jews, the modern nation state of Israel would not exist. He contends that without Hitler, the de-colonisation of former European spheres of influence would have been postponed. Further, Haffner claims that other than Alexander the Great, Hitler had a more significant impact than any other comparable historical figure, in that he too caused a wide range of worldwide changes in a relatively short time span.

"Well, what do you think, Eddie?" Joy asked after few minutes breather.

"Hitler caused the deaths of a lot of people, but maybe some good has come out of it," Eddie pressed with an expression on his face suggesting an expectation of an argument.

"So you're still buying off on Frederic's spiel."

"Well, I'll talk with him about all this and listen to what he has to say." *He will still tell me to kill the Jew bitch when he's ready for me to do it*, he thought.

"Better be careful when you confront him. You could be skating on thin ice."

"Hey, I'm used to that and can take care of myself."

"Before we move on from World War II, we need to cover Japan's role, and I want to share with you Eddie what my father told me about life in the US during that time. Hey, it's near one o'clock. Time for a break, and some lunch. Let's go on over to Godfathers."

Chapter 4 – Japan and US

Tuesday, Oct. 4, 2016, Home of Joyce Levinson, 4:30 PM

Joyce began, "This was cited earlier:"

Germany's formal alliance with Japan and Italy, known collectively as the Axis powers, was signed to deter the United States from supporting and protecting the British.

"Japan's and Italy's expansionist goals motivated them. That signing took place in 1940. It led to the Japanese attack on Pearl Harbor on December 7, 1941. The devastation was terrible. Here are photos from my Pa's scrapbook. The first is of of the ship the Arizona:

The second is the airfield:

The attack put us into World War II. President Franklin Delano Roosevelt addressed the country on radio, calling it, 'a date that will live in infamy.'"

"When I was ten years old I became extremely interested in the World War II period" revealed Joyce," and asked my father, George Landry if he could tell me about it. He was 55 years old at the time."

"Of course my bundle of Joy," he said. "I've long wondered to whom I might one day leave my scrapbook."
"You have a scrapbook, Pa?" I shouted out.

Joy was all the while watching the expressions on Eddie's face. She asked at last, "Would you like me to show you the scrapbook, Eddie?"
"Absolutely, and share with me what he told you?"
"All I can recall."
"Good," he acknowledged, and, forgot for the moment that he was supposed to kill Joy.

Joy placed the scrapbook on the coffee table fronting the couch and sat down next Eddie. She turned to him and said, "I've personally lived through several wars, but none compare with what Pa told me about the reaction of our people during World War II. When he told me it was different and, I asked him how."

"My dear Joy, there was an outpouring of common purpose such as I never saw before or since. Almost overnight, the whole country went onto a war footing. Men of all ages, colors, religions, ancestry wanted to fight for our country. That left jobs in the factories to fill. Women left off being mainly homemakers and filled those jobs, most important because factories were now turning

out tanks, jeeps, and airplanes. Gone were automobile production and anything else not for the war effort."

"That is amazing, Pa."

"It was amazing, Joy and there was reasonable consideration given to men like myself, a few years older with families to look after. Nevertheless, everyone chipped in the best that they could. These posters appeared everywhere:"

"Uncle Sam!" blurted Joy.
"And 'Rosie the Riveter," Pa added.

"Women were greatly respected for their contributions. Also, we all bought war bonds to help fund the war."
"Pa this is a wonderful country," Joy lauded.

"Nothing could stop us, my dear, because we were all working for the common cause. It was great."

"Did everyone want the war to go on forever?"

"Not at all... the downside was our boys killed in Europe and Asia. The country came together in a wonderful way, but the price was very high."

"So, people were happy when it was over."

"There was dancing in the streets. In the town where I lived, people came out of their homes on the news of the war ending in Europe. Not just a few but everyone, dancing and singing, and nobody left out."

"Makes one think what is important, does it not Eddie?"

"Yes... yes, Joy."

Eddie remained quiet a while, but Joy felt she was making progress with him and waited him out silently.

Then, he asked, "What did your Pa say about Japan?"

"I specifically asked him about that."

"What about Japan, Pa"

"Well, that turned out to be a more difficult situation. The first thing you need to know is that the Japanese were not about to give up just because we bested Hitler. We also had a major change in our leadership. Franklin Delano Roosevelt in his fourth term in office died just before the fighting ended in Europe. His vice president, Harry S. Truman, became president."

"Was he a good president, Pa?"

"I think he was, but he had a major dilemma to deal with, Joy."

"Which was?"

"The Japanese were not giving up, and it cost the lives of our soldiers. He had a possible resolution, but it was not a pretty one. Over the period that we had been fighting the war, our scientists at Los Alamos Laboratories in New Mexico learned how to make an atomic bomb. They tested it in the deserts of Nevada as it produced a huge mushroom cloud."

"And you have a picture of that Pa?"

"I do, and here it is."

Joy gasped but remained silent.
    Keep in mind that the situation is in some ways
worse today."
    "Why?"
    "It's because of the number of countries that
have nuclear weapons."
    "Show me the picture Pa, and tell me what
happened with Japan."
    We called them 'Japs' and even Hollywood
made movies like "Destination Tokyo

"Here was the dilemma with Japan. We could continue to fight them with conventional weapons, but the war would drag on for who knew how long. We would lose many of our soldiers. We could, on the other hand, drop atomic bombs on a couple of their major cities to gain their attention. Harry Truman agonized about this briefly but had the support of the on-going anti-Japanese propaganda. Truman ultimately decided to save our soldiers. We sent bombers with atomic bomb payloads, and they did the job at Hiroshima and Nagasaki. The war was over. I don't know what the cost in Japanese lives was, but we were in good shape or so we thought."

"Pa, but you said only Japan was left."

"That's true, but it seems there is always someone out there ready to take advantage of what they perceive as an opportunity. In this case, it was Russia, and this is where we are going to finish. As soon as the hostilities with Germany ended, Russia hurried to expand its control in Europe. They took over one country after another until we laid down the law that they could go no further and the cold war began. That's it."

"Thank you, Pa. I love you."

"That's the end of what I can tell you about Hitler and World War II, Eddie," advised Joyce

"That's a lot of food for thought. Do you have much more to share?"

"You have no idea, my young friend. Tomorrow I will tell of my first personal experience with a Nazi, name of Howard Brooks."

Eddie shook his head in wonderment at Joy's unending source of material. *What would Frederic say if he knew I was listening to all this? Better, for now, he does not know. Maybe have a conversation with Frederic after Joyce tells me about Howard Brooks.*

Chapter 5 – Howard Brooks I

Wednesday, October 5, 2016, Home of Joyce Levinson,
9:00 AM

Eddie and Joyce cleared off the dishes from breakfast into the sink. They left their coffee cups, sugar cube bowl, and a small pitcher of milk. The coffee pot remained on the stove where it would stay warm.

They seated themselves at the table, and Eddie waited for Joy to begin. She seemed to be considering where to start. Then she smiled and began. "It was 1975. I was twenty-two years old when I met Howard Brooks."

"Early in the evening of the day I met him, Howard was on the way to the place of our meeting, THE SPOT, a well-known meeting, and drinking place for singles. He was on the way there at the urging of his apartment neighbor, George Skinner.

George much later shared with me the nature of their travel together that night. George said that Howard was, as usual, his morose self. When George expressed his excitement at the possibilities of meeting some super fun lovin chickees, glum Howard was not so sure. Finally, George chided him for not appreciating George for getting him out his dinky little room and away from his weird collection. George said the next thing he knew; muscular Howard had a large hand around his thin neck. That he, George, was stretched upward and grabbed hold of Howard's arm to ease the pressure on his throat. His tongue pushed out between his lips."

"Then, George said Howard advised, 'George, I'm here with you, and maybe we'll have a grand old time and maybe we won't, but my room is my business.' He then slowly relaxed his grip, and I settled back to the sidewalk. They continued on their way, and George said that the pleasant night conspired against the earlier strain. He put the incident behind him."

"George observed that at thirty-three, Howard Brooks was a quiet, morose individual, a repeated failure with women. It was no wonder he had more doubts than George about the turn out of the evening. The first impression was that Howard was stocky. On closer examination, one could determine that he was more muscular than fat with a six foot, two-inch frame."

"Then they were almost there. A fringed gold awning projected forward on the sidewalk from the street level entrance. A neon sign proclaimed, "Lounge Dancing.""

"George said he looked around while Howard ordered draft beers. George said when he returned, he took a swallow of the draft and asked Howard, 'How'd you like to meet a golden hair beauty, named Joy?'"

"He was, of course, referring to me," said Joyce.

Eddie smiled and confirmed, "Of course."

"I was there with Ann Damiano who shared an apartment with me. George told me later that it was almost too much for insecure Howard. He wanted me but would I want him?"

"'Howard,' I began, 'I just moved in with Ann. Isn't she terrific? My family lives in Medford. I work at Massachusetts Bay Mutual, near here,' I told him.''

"'I know where it is,' Howard said and added, 'I'm a driver for Spartan Movers in Cambridge.'''

"From there, Eddie, our conversation went like this:''

"He, ya know? You look like you could be a truck driver. I mean you're big, and look strong. Do you drive all over?"

"Mostly it's local moves. Sometimes to other places."

"Do you like it?"

"Look, it's a job. I'm not into it all that much."

"Oh, I'm sorry. You're quiet, aren't you, sort of a private person. That's OK. I talk enough for three. And you're not bad looking. I like your being big. I'll bet you're strong."

"I lift weights."

"That's great. I mean physical exercise is good. Let's you get things out of your system. I play tennis, and sometimes I jog. One day I jogged from where I live down to Cleveland Circle and all around the reservoir. I didn't think I was going to make it back, but I did. Well, I cheated a little. I came back on the MBTA. But Boston is great. There are so many cities that you read about these days where you have to be very careful wherever you go. In Boston, there's so much to do, and you can jog or do whatever your thing is, and it's OK. I mean it's not perfect, but it's a good place. What else do you do?"

"I...I collect things."

" What sorts of things?"

"Come over, and I'll show you."

"I'd like to. That'd be fun."

"No, I mean now. Come now, and I'll show you."

"Howie, you're smooth. Quiet but always thinking. I'd love to Hon, but we just met. Why don't you tell me about your collection? I'm very interested, and I like you. Come on," she said leaning very close, "tell me about it."

"If you're interested and like me, you'll come with me."

"Of course I meant what I said, but let's not rush things. After we get to know one another a little better, I'll come over."

"Forget it. I knew you didn't mean all this business about being interested and liking me. It's crap."

"Now, in endeavoring to dissuade Howard, I passed the point of easy retreat. 'Look, Howard, it isn't even practical. How would we get there? You came with George didn't you?'"

"Howard sensed he was winning. 'MBTA, I live a block from the streetcar line. Come, or you're a phony...'

'Gees, I must be crazy. Just to see your collection?'"

"'Yeah,' he responded."

"'Hang on while I tell Ann and George.' I advised."

"I could tell Howard watched as I made my way to the dance floor. He saw George and Ann nodding as I spoke."

"'OK, let's go,' I said when I returned. 'I've heard a lot of stories, and I still don't know why I'm doing this. George said he didn't think I'd care for your collection but that's between you and me. He said you're not a rapist or anything.'"

"Several times Howard asked me to be open minded about his collection or it was all going to be a waste. I kept telling him not to worry. Not to be uptight about it.

I understood that this was something important to him. And I began to realize that Howard had something to show me, Eddie."

"Howard lived in a sturdy 3 three story brick apartment building of early nineteen hundreds vintage. If you counted the two-thirds above street level basement, it was four stories high. The front exterior was of white cement blocks to the level of the windows on the first floor. From there up, the exterior was red brick. The double door entryway was at sidewalk height with four windows above at each level. To the right, and left of this center section, the building protruded in the shape of three sides of an octagon. The effect was roughly that of semi-circular turrets at the extremes. The center entry had three columns on each side of the doors, one real and two part of the front facade. They were fluted and had ornate adornment of leaves and scrolls at the top in the style of Roman Corinthian."

On entering, Howard reminded, "Promise to be open."

"I told him to stop worrying."

"Howard opened one of the two large glass doors framed in dark wood. Inside the floor and walls were finished in marble with the mailboxes built into the walls. Large junk mail envelopes and magazines overflowed the drop slot on several of them. It was three or steps up to the level of an interior door which Howard had to unlock. A short distance forward in the hallway we began climbing the well-grooved steps up. The smells of seventy years of living were now part of the walls."

"Howard's studio apartment was on the second floor level towards the rear. Howard fumbled with the key for a moment and then with some resolve unlocked the door.

He let it swing open so I could enter. I didn't know what to expect but didn't expect to be shocked. I had begun to feel Howard was exaggerating the whole thing. As the door swung open, a torrent of red, white and black struck me. The effect did not lessen as I more fully entered the room. I was face to face with a wall-size reproduction of a Nazi swastika flag, a huge twisted black cross on a white circular background itself on scarlet background that completed the wall.

"Was it a creek in the floor, a sound from Howard's physiology or something in my head that revived me?"

"'I made it myself,' he said. 'The angles and proportions are perfect. The white and black were easy but getting the exact red took me weeks. I laid it out with pencil first. Well, before even, I had to work the wall. You know to get it smooth. See. If you look close there, you can see where I patched and sanded it smooth. But it was worth it. It's perfect.' His eyes were distant as he closed the door. He hardly seemed to be aware of me. Here was his fascination, the reality and LIFE."

"So," said Joy, "Howard was in his element, and there was I, hit by a swastika thunderbolt, Eddie."

"Let me continue the account of what happened. We'll do something about lunch following this."

Eddie nodded his agreement.

"Here we go signaled Joy. Howard went from the swastika to another proud item.

"Look!" he shouted pointing to a poster on an adjacent wall.

"Howard then excitedly drew my attention to a Luger automatic pistol and other treasures in his collection."

"I knew at once I made a large mistake. I had to get away but had to be careful not to offend Howard. I didn't pull it off."

"Howard's manic excitement turned into uncontrolled rage. He suddenly grabbed me. I struggled to get free, but he was too strong. However, at the decisive moment, he released his grip on me and allowed me to leave."

"Later in my apartment in Cambridge and shaken I told my roommate, Ann Damiano, about my experience."

"There was a giant swastika in full color, on one wall, a huge Hitler poster on another and a Luger pistol on special display on a counter along with many other frightening objects. He was in a rage about my reaction, and I thought he was going to kill me. Maybe we should report him to the police."

"'Let's do it,' encouraged Ann."

"We called the local police station, and they said they were immediately dispatching a policeman to our apartment."

"Officer O'Brien showed up twenty minutes later and patiently listened to everything I had to say."

"He may be dangerous," assessed O'Brien. "However, he's not breaking any laws by collecting Nazi paraphernalia, Joy. You could swear out an assault complaint, but it would be your word against Howard's."

"I agreed it was better not to pursue it, but I didn't sleep well that night. Let' have our late lunch, Eddie. I have already prepared ham and Swiss cheese sandwiches, potato salad and non-dill pickles, she underscored."

Joy put out the food along with CocaCola over ice. She placed an uncut pumpkin pie on a nearby counter for later dessert.

They munched silently for a bit and then Eddie volunteered, "I can understand that you were taken back by the poster and swastika because you schooled in the belief they have to be bad. That does not necessarily have to be correct especially here in 2016. Howard was breaking ground and probably got himself into trouble." *Have to touch base with Frederic,* he thought.

"Well, he did, and we'll cover more about that," Joy responded. "I have much more of importance to share with you and am ready to give you a Frederic break anytime you need to do that."

"Yes," Eddie responded simply in a subdued manner. *I know she thinks she's helping me but she's behind the times. I'll just have to see this to the end. Maybe I won't have to kill her. Frederic will help me to do the right thing.*

Wednesday, October 5, 2016, Home of Joyce Levinson, 3:00 PM

Following lunch, Joy suggested continuing on Howard Brooks in the living room. They took their usual seats.

"Shall I continue with the Howard Brooks saga, Eddie?" asked Joy.

"Let's have it," acknowledged Eddie.

"This is what happened. Unsettled from the latest failure with women, and that would have been me, Howard, in his responsibility for Spartan movers, had a scheduled pickup in Cambridge. Howard and his two helpers arrived at Sadie Berger's apartment in Brookline to find nothing packed. Sadie explained that she's a very old lady and thought it was all included. She emphasized she couldn't pack it all by herself if she wanted to do it."

There it was again. At the source of everything that's was always wrong in Howard's life. Jews! The apartment smells, Sadie's old, wrinkled Jewish face and her Yiddish accent revolted him. With the unplanned packing, they couldn't complete the move until later than planned. It was almost more than he could bear.

However, by early afternoon, they were almost done with loading the truck, but Sadie learned they were not planning on taking the refrigerator. Howard explained that it was not on the manifest. And he' wasn't taking it. Maybe it belongs to the apartment, he reasoned. How does he know it's hers. And they're late already. She'll have to have somebody else move it later. How he hates the old Jew bitch.

Crying and hollering, Sadie refuses to let them go without her refrigerator. He tells one the workers that if they happen to push her out of the way, maybe she'll fall and crack her head open. Better yet, maybe a heart attack would take her. One of the helpers intervenes. He called the office. They're to take the refrigerator.

Chapter 6 – Howard Brooks II

Thurs. Oct. 6, 2016, Home of Joyce Levinson, 9:30 AM

Having finished breakfast and cleared the table, Joy continued with the Howard Brooks story.

"Eddie," Joy began, "I need to introduce a new player in this saga. His name is Milt Greene, the Spartan Movers Operations Manager.

Remember, Eddie, this took place in 1975 and Milt, at that time, lived in Newton, Massachusetts, once the most affluent suburbs outside of Boston. Not quite so anymore but still a good place to live. It was a whole kind of life different than what Milt grew up with in the Dorchester of the '40s and 50s. It was a long way up, but he and his family had a good life. The day I'm going relate to you, Eddie, was a difficult one. We're moving to the Sadie Berger incident, and Milt's talk with Howard about it. The news for Howard was going to be bad. According to police reports published later in the press, this the way it went."

"Howard, I'm letting you go," Milt advised. "That refrigerator business was too much. Bad for business. Maybe you ought to think about getting into something else. You can collect if you want. I won't fight it. I'm sorry it had to come to this."

"Howard angrily responded, 'Screw all of you bastards,' and he left in a huff. He later told police that he spent the rest of the day working out at the gym and planning for his and his father's day of revenge. He admitted he totally lost it."

"On returning to his home, Howard encountered George Skinner who later reported that with no one else to whom to complain, he spewed on George. George admitted he was afraid of Howard and listened as Howard vented his upset."

"The Jews and niggers are ruining everything," he disgorged. "Where does a slimy Jew get off in firing me? Hitler was right. God, why didn't he have enough time to wipe them out? They're ruining everything."

"George said later that he tried to calm Howard, without success. Howard continued his rant."

"The whole thing is repeating, with this Greene. Greene? Ha! What is it? Greenberg? Or Greenstein? It isn't going to end here. If I had him here now, I would reach for Milt's throat and squeeze until his tongue moved no more."

"George, knew well the seriousness of Howard's threat, that he only needed some time to plan and do it right."

"The newspaper coverage later divulged that Howard waited in the morning until he was sure everyone would be in at Spartan, especially Milt. Howard loaded up his

Lugar, automatic rifle, bullets, and grenades and was
ready to go. Arriving about 8:15 am, Howard parked
briefly down the street from Spartan and waited until he
saw no one near the worker's office entrance. He then
moved and parked close. He later, via phone, bragged to
police about his entry into the building."

*"The entrance hallway was dim. Up a half-flight of
stairs at the end connected with the main office hallway.
I proceeded to the entrance end. Then, up the stairs to the
office hallway, and a right turn to the general office area.
I swung the door open. The night man was there and*
BOOM! *My gun exploded. I unexpectedly shot the
night watchman, didn't even think about it. Then up the
stairs into another hallway.* **BOOM!** *I shot D'Antonio,
the owner.* **BOOM! BOOM!** *I shot Mrs. Hartwell,
D'Antonio's secretary, and Shrank, the controller! They
should've stayed in their offices.*

*I finally reached the general office area. The workers
inside, reversed their motion toward the door as I busted
in, automatic rifle in my hands. Everyone froze while I
moved into Milt's office which had windows and
connected only with the general office area. I was near
taking a fit when someone said that Milt was out in the
garage or yard.*

I herded my four hostages into Milt's office and waited.

"The four hostages," advised Joyce, as she handed a
print out to Eddie, "were later described as:"

Paula Miles-*General office secretary, 32 years old, married, lives with husband at Coolidge Towers high-rise apartments in Brookline, no children, native of Lowell, competent, confident, quasi-career type.*

Harry Thompson—*In charge of scheduling and complaints, 52 years old, three daughters, grown up and married, owns a four-family house in Maiden, lives with wife of 30 years, an old pro in moving business, became inside-man after a heart attack four years earlier.*

Steve D'Antonio — *Summer Office help, 16 years old, son of the owner, lives in Arlington with parents and younger sister, two older brothers are outside Spartan workers.*

Sara Weeks - *18-year-old black girl, lives with a grandmother in Jamaica Plains with both parents dead in an automobile accident seven years earlier, timid, thin, plain, competent.*

"Here is the police account of what happened next and as published in the press," Joyce said as she handed Eddie another document from which she immediately began reading..."

From the window in Milt s office, Howard watched what was going on in the garage. He kept his prisoners in the other end of the office hands over heads facing and leaning against the wall. He observed the receptionist, Sally, running to speak with Don Davis, a driver for Spartan. The phone rang. The police advised Howard that they were outside and he should give himself up. He

*told them to send in Milt Greene, "Send in the Jew."
Police advised they would talk with Milt and call him.*

*Howard observed as workers fled the garage. Via the
door controls in Milt's office, he closed all doors sealing
off entry from there. The police reported that Milt
wouldn't walk into certain death. Howard told them it
was up to them and the Jew. If he doesn't come in, they'd
have four dead hostages on their heads. The police
explained that they couldn't force Milt Greene to go in if
he refused. Howard told them to figure something out, or
he's was going to start killing hostages and Sara Weeks
would probably be first. He hung up on the police.*

*The police came up with a deal. Milt would come into the
garage area. Howard could raise one of the doors, let
him enter, close the doors sealing him in, then have at
him. Howard asked how he'd know whether Milt would
be armed and wouldn't the police move in once he gave
up the hostages? It was the only deal they could make.
Milt wasn't going to walk into certain death, and if he
wanted a chance to have at him, it's was the best they
could do. Howard agreed to the terms.*

*Milt came into the garage. Howard smashed the electric
controls once the door closed. He marched the prisoners
out of Milt's office and lined them up in front of him with
his back to the door leading to the garage. Paula Miles
was at the front of the line, then Harry Thompson, Steve
D'Antonio and finally Sara Weeks. He released them one
at a time through the door to the office hallway. At the
last moment, as Sara prepared to follow the others,
Howard grabbed her wrist and shouted to the police that*

he was going after the Jew. And if they followed, the black cunt was going to be dead. Once in the garage, Howard began moving toward the area in front of Door 1. All the while he dragged Sara after him by the wrist. Howard saw the general office area door open and shouted that Sara would be dead as he fired a shot at the door. It quickly closed. The Jew was hiding somewhere but where? Perhaps in the car parked in front of Door 1. He opened the door, stepped up and looked in. Empty. Howard turned on the CB radio. Maybe he'd hear something about what was happening at Spartan. Milt's voice talking to the police is what he heard. Milt was at the far end of the garage hiding in a cab in front of Door 6. The police had just about repaired the controls for the door, and Milt was going to make a run for it. Howard pulled Sara into the closest cab after him, slammed the door and started the motor. At the far end, a garage door was already opening, and Milt had started the engine in his cab too.

Milt tore out of the garage grazing the top of the cab on the lower part of the still rising door. Howard was right behind. Milt sped out of the yard with Howard in hot pursuit. The police were afraid to take any action that could cause Howard to shoot Sara. Milt would have to stay ahead of Howard until the police could find an opening or until Howard caught him.

Police were afraid to interfere in the chase until there was an opening. The plan was to follow close, see what developed.

A high speed, harrowing chase took place on local streets of Cambridge across the Mass. Ave. Bridge into Boston with police following at a safe distance and looking for an opening. The chase continued on local streets of Boston and onto the Expressway south. At a traffic slowdown due to construction, Milt got off in Dorchester and tried to lose his pursuer on local roads nearby the ocean front. Aware that the police were not far behind and sensed he was closing in for the kill, Howard stopped police by dropping a grenade behind as he sped after Milt. On the ride, Sara remembered the awful details of the last ride with her parents and the terrible accident that only she survived. Perhaps it was ordained that this would be her end too. If not, perhaps it would be a sign that her parent's death was in the past and something to put away.

Milt finally stopped near the ocean with no place to go and Howard closing fast. Milt had the gun the police gave him. God knows he was the last person in the world who should have to save himself with a gun. But better to go trying. With the truck stopped now, he'd stand on the step of the truck and take careful aim back over the open door. Maybe he'd be lucky. He'd try to keep from hurting Sara but what else could he do? Milt maneuvered into position. Howard was too fast. The impact of Howard's cab, hitting his, threw the gun loose and back. Milt, dazed and hurt fell to the ground.

With the Luger in one hand and dragging Sara with the other hand, Howard leeped from the cab. "Now, You're dead," he said.

As Howard approached, he saw that Milt was not going to be able to put up much of a fight. There would be one less Jew in the world but one way or another it would be his end too, so why not savor the moment. No sense in ending it too quick. Howard threw Sara to the ground as he released her and advanced toward Milt. Badly shaken but aware that he was struggling for his life, Milt staggered to his feet. Howard whipped the Luger across Milt's face sending him down. This time Howard was going to have the pleasure of Milt's pain' as he broke his body. He kicked Milt fiercely in the midsection. He yanked him from the ground and prepared to work on his face, now bleeding from the corner of his mouth.

"I-i-i-i-e-e-e-e-e," Sara screamed as she pulled the trigger on Milt's gun. Howard with eyes glazed turned and only began a motion toward her. Sara held the gun still in both hands, and with tears streaming down her face, fired three more shots in succession. Howard was no more."

Later, Sara visited with Milt in the hospital. He told her that he understood that she saved his life and he was grateful for her courage. She told Milt that the newspapers were saying that she was a hero but how do people get so twisted and with people being killed and hurt? She cried softly, and she muttered, "Nobody wins."

"Was Sara right, 'Nobody Wins' Eddie?" queried Joyce.

"Sometimes sacrifice is necessary," offered, Eddie.

Changing the subject, Joyce advised, "Interestingly, a couple of years after my experience with Howard Brooks, a similar incident surfaced in New Rochelle, New York. The central character was Frederick William Cowan. It did not personally involve me, but the parallels with my experience were striking. So Frederick William Cowan will be the next subject I will share with you. Here's a photo of him:"

"Wow! Big Guy," Eddie exclaimed.

"Yes, he was," acknowledged Joy. "Now, by the way, is a good time for you to take a break to visit with your Frederic. So why don't you take a day or two to confer with him. I'm flexible and if a meeting with Frederic doesn't work out, come right back here, and I'll fill you in on the 1977 escapades of Frederick William Cowan."

"Thank you, Joy."

Allen Pollens

Chapter 7 – Frederic & Frederick

Friday, Oct. 7, 2016, Offices of Oregon Feistys, 9:30 AM

Eddie rang the bell at the Oregon Feistys.

"Who is it?" a male voice asked. It was Frederic Fiester, the Feistys leader.

"It's me, Eddie, Frederic." He then heard Frederic removing the chain and unlocking the door.

The door opened, and there, as usual, stood Frederic Feister wth a smile on his face.

He stepped forward and hugged Eddie in a warm embrace even as he expressed, "Welcome Eddie I'm glad you came by."

Frederic was tall and muscular, towered over Eddie. He placed his arm around and onto Eddie's shoulder even as he ushered Eddie into the large open space.

Everything looked about the same as in his last visit. There was the portrait of Hitler.

Publisher: Kunstanstalten May

There was also the large cloth mounted swastika.

"The crew is out on assignment," Frederic explained, "so we have the whole office to ourselves."

Frederic sat down with Eddie on the couch located in the corner of the large room. He set out a bottle and two glasses on the small table that fronted the sofa. "Have some Schnapps with me, Eddie," he suggested.

"Of course," responded Eddie.

While Frederic filled their glasses with the brew, he asked, "How does it go with Mrs. Levinson?" emphasizing *Levinson.*

"We're still going down the road of her sharing her personal Nazi experiences. She has a lot to say."

"Nature of the Jew," commented Frederic.

Except she denies being a Jew, thought Eddie. "Has anything changed here, Frederic?"

"No, we have the same game plan, and I have to ask you to tough it out until the time is right. Keep listening to the stories and nodding your head. Can you do that?"

"Y-yes, I can do that." Eddie decided to change the subject. "Have you been to Germany? You told me once it's where your father was from."

"Yes, and yes, Wonderful visits in Berlin and Munich. My father came from Germany after war."

"How was he able to do that?"

"It was ironic that this country valued his experience as a Nazi and wanted him to spy in Europe for the US."

They talked at some length about their backgrounds and values while sharing a Schnapps refill.

Frederic closed saying, "I like you Eddie and am proud of the way you established yourself with the Jew."

He thanked Frederic and with a warm hug left, thinking, *I hope we're doing the right thing, Frederic.*

It was past noon when Eddie arrived at Joy's house.

"Come on in," she welcomed him enthusiastically.

"Are you hungry? Follow me," she urged without waiting for an answer.

He tracked after into the kitchen where the table was set out for lunch.

"Chinese everything courtesy of Chen's delivery," Joy said.

"I don't want it to spoil your breakfast but the subject for this morning is Frederick William Cowan," Joyce said but before we talk about Cowan - how did your meeting with Frederic Feister go?" Joyce asked as she seated herself. "Oh, and help yourself from Chen's offerings in the white boxes." She watched as Eddie loaded up his plate with rice, noodles, and Orange Chicken. Then she did the same.

"I put out both chopsticks and regular utensils. Use whatever you like to use." She proceeded with the chopsticks. "Frederic Fiester?" she reminded.

"Oh, he had a bunch of stuff he's doing and encouraged me to hear you out on what you know about Nazism and all."

Eddie, as usual, began eating ravenously, while muttering, "Delicious, I love this."

"Still thinks I'm Jewish and should not be allowed to live?"

Eddie choked on his food and then struggled to speak, "He.., he.., has other things on his mind, right now. We didn't talk about you," he lied.

Joy decided to drop the subject and subsequently advised, "As I mentioned, the subject for this morning is Frederick William Cowan. In 1977, about two years after my experience with Howard Brooks, I was shocked to learn of a similar episode in New Rochelle, New York. Here," she said, "from Murderpedia online is a printout of the important coverage. Look it over, and we'll talk about it after lunch, in the living room, OK?"

Eddie nodded his agreement.

Subsequently, in the living room, Joyce read aloud the initial paragraph:

Frederick William Cowan

A hardworking ex-GI, Freddie lived with his parents and fantasized about being "like Hitler." He kept a collection of Nazi weapons and other memorabilia and enjoyed wearing his German tanker helmet and pretending he was in the SS. In one of his Nazi books found by authorities in his attic bedroom he had written: "There is nothing lower than black and Jewish people unless it's the police who protect them."

"This," added Joyce, "is exactly the kind of person who should not be allowed to have guns, First Amendment or not."

"First Amendment?" puzzled Eddie.

"In the United States Constitution, the so-called, *right to bear arms,* the ultimate protection against a government gone wrong.

"Oh," was Eddie's short response. *Have to think about this.*

Joyce continued reading from the printout.

Scheduled to Resume Work

Mr. Cowan, the son of a retired postal worker, lived at 40 Woodbury Avenue with his parents, William and Dorothy Cowan, and two brothers. He had been scheduled to resume his regular work yesterday at the expiration of his suspension by a supervisor, Norman Bing.

It was shortly before 8 A.M. when he arrived at Neptune's office and warehouse complex at 55 Weyman Avenue in a largely commercial and working class residential section on the southern edge of New Rochelle. Warehouses, a lumber yard, and gasoline stations dot the area, which crisscrosses Interstate 95, the tracks of Conrail's New Haven division and some streets.

The Neptune complex, where upwards of 300 people are employed, consists of a two-story, tinted- glass office building at the front, and a block-long garage and warehouse at the rear, where dozens of tractor trailer trucks are nosed up in long rows, appearing from overhead like the legs of a giant centipede.

Mr. Cowan drove up at 7:45 A.M., according to some witnesses, and took several weapons out of the trunk of his car, which he left in the parking lot. He then walked into the ground-floor vestibule of the office section, making no effort to hide his weapons.

"It's obvious where this is going," commented Joyce.

Eddie knew she was right but remained silent. Joyce continued.

He shot two fellow employees dead in the vestibule, each with a bullet in the chest. "He got them point blank," said Clynt Wynent, who was punching a time clock. "They weren't moving. They looked dead."

The First 3 Victims

The first two men killed were Joseph Hicks, 60, of 11 Park Avenue, Mount Vernon, and Frederick Holmes, 55, of 871 East 219th Street, the Bronx. Both were company employees, and both were black.

James Green, 45, also black, was the next to die. A company mover, he lived at 616 Lincoln Avenue, Mount Vernon. He was standing a short distance from the time clock, witnesses said, and turned to run when he saw the first two victims fall. Mr. Cowan shot Mr. Green in the back, and he fell dead on a flight of stairs leading to the second floor.

"You see," commented, Joyce, "no hesitation there. They were black."

Eddie continued silent, was content for Joyce to be reading.

At least two other employees were threatened, according to Police Commissioner Hagerty. Mr. Cowan put his rifle to their faces before letting them flee.

Ronald Cowell, 39, was one of them. "I had one foot out the door, and I was staring at the muzzle of the rifle he was carrying." He recalled. "I started saying, 'Please,' and he said: 'Go home and tell my mother not to come down to Neptune.' I didn't look back. I just kept on running."

Witnesses said Mr. Cowan shouted for Norman Bing, the supervisor who had suspended him, but Mr. Bing hid for several hours in the building and he was not hurt. But apparently searching for Mr. Bing, the gunman marched toward the building's ground-floor cafeteria, where workers were having coffee. Edward Miller, one of the workers inside, said, "Mr. Cowan fired a blast through the cafeteria door, and we ran."

With another gunshot into the cafeteria, Mr. Cowan killed 32-year-old Pariyarathu Varghese, an electrician, of 80 Guion Place, New Rochelle, who moved to this country from India last November and began work with Neptune only last week.

"Of course," put in Joyce, "a clear Nazi choice. Do you see how ugly and sick this is? Oh, I'm sorry, you're probably still wrestling with all this."

Joyce will never understand, he thought. Eddie allowed Joyce to continue.

As others fled from the cafeteria, Mr. Cowan walked out and strode upstairs to take up a firing position on the second floor. Soon the police began pulling up outside.

Warning Came Too Late

A New Rochelle police officer, Allen McLeod, 29, was one of the first to arrive, at about 8:15 A.M. Witnesses said that one of the workers who had fled from the building shouted to the policeman to warn him of the possible sniper fire just as he stepped out of his car, but it was too late.

He was killed on the spot by a bullet fired from a second-floor window by Mr. Cowan. Officer McLeod, who was married and the father of two children, lived at 17 Addison Street in Larchmont.

"A white man!" exclaimed Joyce.

"He was an enemy at this point," Eddie responded.

Joyce decided not to challenge him and continued reading

Three other New Rochelle policemen who arrived shortly afterward were wounded by Mr. Cowan's gunfire. They were Officer Raymond Satiro, who suffered a leg wound; Officer John Fitzgibbon, who sustained a hand wound, and Lieut. Vincent Fontanarosa, who was wounded in the arm. Officer Fitzgibbon and Lieutenant Fontanarosa were released after treatment at New Rochelle Hospital.

Inside the building, two company employees had been wounded by the gunman. Joseph Russo, of 137 Beechman Avenue, Mount Vernon, suffered a critical gunshot wound to the abdomen, and Robert Harris sustained an eye wound that did not require hospitalization.

Joyce decided to withhold a further comment. It would ultimately be up to Eddie to reason this out. She went on.

While several employees hid inside, dozens of others escaped before the arrival of the police. The police cordoned off a two-block section of Weyman Avenue, set up sharpshooters on nearby roofs and a command post in a grocery supply warehouse next door and began summoning reinforcements.

The gunman, a 250-pound, 6-foot man who had worked for about ten years for Neptune, exchanged gunfire with the police for nearly an hour. His gunshots struck police cars, private automobiles and moving vans, shattered windows in an unoccupied school across the street and other buildings two blocks away and sent police officers dashing for cover, unable to reach the dead and wounded.

Police sharpshooters in flak vests returned the fire but were frustrated because the gunman could see them through the building's tinted windows, but they could not see him moving around inside on the second floor.

Copters Circle Overhead

Four state police helicopters were soon circling overhead, and by 10 A.M., a tank-like armored personnel carrier from New York City's Police Department moved onto the scene. It was used as a shield to retrieve the body of Officer McLeod. The body had been lying in the open, and the police had been unable to get close without exposing them to the gunman's telescopic sight.

"Frederick certainly gained attention but where in the devil did he think this was going?" interrupted Joyce.

"Nowhere, Joyce, but he still hadn't found Bing, and he was in the middle of a stirred up hornet's nest. I'll read for a bit."

The gunman, who at various times was inside the office or on its roof, shouted that he had "plenty of grenades and other guns to last me all day," and it was unclear whether he was holding any hostages. During the

*morning and early afternoon, some employees who had
hidden inside ran out to safety.*

*As the siege wore on, a hostage negotiating team from
New York City arrived, but they were unable to make
contact with the gunman.*

*A loudspeaker on the armored personnel carrier was
used to address him, and he was repeatedly given the
telephone number of the police command post to call.*

*At about 11 A.M., his parents and two brothers were
brought up to make appeals for his surrender, but the
attempt met with silence.*

*"Pray for Freddie," his mother told a friend. "He's gone
crazy."*

"They were certainly right about that!" voiced Joyce.
Eddie decided that it was hard enough for him to
reconcile and not to respond to Joy's obvious upset. He
continued with the printout.

Cowan Phones Police

*About noon, Mr. Cowan did telephone the police
command post. He made no demands, other than for hot
chocolate and potato salad, and asked that his apologies
for the "trouble" be conveyed to the Mayor. No lunch was
sent in.*

Lunch and an apology to the mayor. Eddie realized
how far out of it Cowan was but did not comment.

*About 300 policemen were involved in the siege.
Commissioner Hagerty said that between 20 and 25
employees were believed to have been hiding in the
building. Only one, a man hiding in a second-floor
bathroom, remained trapped all day.*

*"That's why we haven't rushed the place as yet —
because there are people still in there," Mayor Rippa told
reporters at the scene.*

*"We are trying to initiate negotiations." Commissioner
Hagerty said. "We have tried telephone communications.
We have tried speaking through air-conditioning
conducts. We have tried direct personal communications.
So far we have been unable to communicate."*

*By midafternoon, the siege had attracted large crowds to
nearby streets and rooftops. Police barricades were set
up to keep crowds back.*

"It certainly, at that point, had to be obvious to
Frederick that he was in a no-win situation for all that he
had done," assessed Joyce.

"Yes," was Eddie's terse response as he went on.

*Mr. Cowan was holed up in an office on the north side of
the building's second floor when he shot himself dead
through the right temple. Several hours later, when the
police moved onto the second floor with dogs, Mr. Cowan
was found face down, a .45-caliber Colt pistol in his right
hand and a Browning 9-milimeter pistol on the floor
beside him.*

On a nearby table, there were two other handguns. The rifle Mr. Cowan had used was leaning against a chair, and 200 rounds of ammunition for it were lying nearby.

Joyce finished reading this last part of the account aloud.

In the police search of Cowan's attic apartment on February 14, they found a thick metal belt buckle among his belongings. Inscribed boldly on the front of that buckle were these prophetic words: "I will give up my gun when they pry my cold dead fingers from around it!"

"What do you think, Eddie?" Joy asked,
"Well, he went crazy."
"And it was a Nazi thing," she underscored
Eddie shrugged, and Joyce decided not to pursue it considering they were only up to 1977. There was much more up ahead.

Allen Pollens

Chapter 8 – A Flawed Species

Sat., Oct. 8, 2016, Home of Joyce Levinson, 10:00 AM

Eddie raced out of the guest room that Joyce had made available to him. He found Joyce in the kitchen busily preparing some food.

"I am so sorry," he said, "I somehow overslept."
"No, you are fine. Do you remember me looking in on you a little about two hours ago and telling you to get some more rest?"
"No."
"You looked fatigued, and that's what I told you. It's Saturday, and you've had a challenging week. You came just in time. How'd coffee and a stack of five buttermilk pancakes do you?"
"Yum," Eddie responded wide-eyed and smiled.
"Plus a couple of strips of crispy bacon?"
"Yum. Yum. Yum!" Eddie advised.

After putting out Eddie's food, Joyce put out some of the same fixings for herself and joined Eddie at the table. She had a new game plan for the day and wondered what Eddie was thinking.

Allen Pollens

Gotta be careful, went through his mind. *She is so generous and kind, how could I hold being Jew against her even if she was?*

Joyce had been looking ahead at what had been developing worldwide in the past forty years. It was deeply disturbing and showed no signs of abating. Here she was trying to save Eddie from losing himself in hatred when she realized that, as crazy as it was, the movements kept surfacing and, that it took only a few, many times just one armed disturbed individual to do something terrible. She decided to have an open conversation with Eddie about this before going further.

She waited until they were done with breakfast and had moved to their usual places in the living room – Joyce in the large armchair and Eddie seated on the couch.

Eddie offered, "I'm feeling lucky, Joy, may I call you, Joy?"

"Of course, my young friend," she responded

"As I was saying, lucky – with a nice place to sleep, wonderful food, and your kindness."

"Ready to give up on The Fiesty's?"

Eddie realized he had gone too far. He thought *Frederic was the one who rescued me from the hole I was in.* "I can't do that, Joyce," he responded. "I like you and all, and what you have covered up to 1977, is interesting. However, this is 2016..."

He was right, and Joyce decided to lay out the nature of the situation. "First, Eddie, I will tell you everything pertinent to 2016. However, the realization struck me that it will not be worth anything unless viewed in the context of the nature of human beings."

The statement took Eddie by surprise, was way more than what he ever considered. He felt Joy was taking him down a road that was only going to add to his confusion. He remained silent.

Joy knew she was treading on a path where she might lose Eddie but felt there was not another course. She plunged in.

"In going forward and researching where these, forgive me, 'HATE' organizations have gone and are going, I realize, what I tell you, wants a longer, bigger view. Please consider the violence that predated Hitler and Nazism. With the birth of the 'one true god' religion came another basis for division and killing which has gone on for 2000 years. Do we need to go back further in time to study human needs to find fault with one another?"

Eddie still didn't know where this was leading but shook his head.

"Good acknowledged," Joyce. "It would be nice if we all appreciated one another as human beings, fortunate to have the precious gift of life. My demised husband, John, would often say, 'We should all be as one.'"

He didn't know my stepfather Morris, went through Eddie's mind. Eddie had not the slightest idea as to where all this was going but nodded his acceptance.

"There were wars and other violence between people as far back as my research would allow, So," assessed Joyce, "you see, we can't expect too much of the flawed

species that we are. However, wholesale murder should
be beyond toleration. With that as a starting point let's
go forward from 1977, okay."

*I could tell you a thing or two about the ugliness of
people to one another,* thought Eddie but he just nodded
to Joyce to continue.

Joyce suddenly sat up straight. "Before we go
forward, we should go back, or we'll miss out on one of
the worst tragedies ever rained down on people in our
country and how it came to a place in our country that
nearly split us in two and on more than one occasion. Do
you have any idea what I'm talking about?"

"No, Joyce."

Joyce opened up her laptop and began a search while
Eddie waited patiently. Finally, she sent an excerpt from
a Wikipedia article to her printer and printed out two
copies. Upon retrieving the documents, she said before
beginning the reading, "I guess what we did to blacks
was not exactly a holocaust. We didn't kill them, just
enslaved them. Was that the beginning of 'White
Supremacy,' one with profit motivation? I guess so."
She began reading, reminding first that it was from
Wikipedia.

*By 1860, there were 3.5 to 4.4 million enslaved African
Americans in the United States due to the Atlantic slave
trade, and another 488,000–500,000 African Americans
lived free (with legislated limits) across the country.*

*The slaves not only constituted a large investment, but
they also produced America's most valuable product and*

*export: cotton. They not only helped build the U.S.
Capitol, but they also built the White House and other
District of Columbia buildings. (Washington was a slave
trading center.) Similar building projects existed in
slaveholding states.*

"Was this 'White Supremacy' on an enormous scale,
Eddie?" queried Joyce.

"We didn't kill them," commented Eddie.

"Was this maybe worse? Maybe there would not be
so much hate directed at blacks if we enslaved them
again, Jews as well?"

Eddie shrugged.

Joy continued reading.

*In 1863, during the American Civil War, President
Abraham Lincoln signed the Emancipation Proclamation.*

The proclamation declared that all slaves in the Confederate-held territory were free. Advancing Union troops enforced the proclamation with Texas being the last state to be emancipated, in 1865.

Slavery in Union-held Confederate territory continued, at least on paper, until the passage of the Thirteenth Amendment in 1865.

Reconstruction Era and Jim Crow

African Americans quickly set up congregations for themselves, as well as schools and community/civic associations, to have space away from white control or oversight. While the post-war Reconstruction era was initially a time of progress for African Americans, that period ended in 1876. By the late 1890s, Southern states enacted Jim Crow laws to enforce racial segregation and disenfranchisement. Most African Americans obeyed the Jim Crow laws, to avoid racially motivated violence. To maintain self-esteem and dignity, African Americans such as Anthony Overton and Mary McLeod Bethune continued to build their own schools, churches, banks, social clubs, and other businesses.

In the last decade of the 19th century, racially discriminatory laws and racial violence aimed at African Americans began to mushroom in the United States These discriminatory acts included racial segregation— upheld by the United States Supreme Court decision in Plessy v. Ferguson in 1896—which was legally mandated by southern states and nationwide at the local level of government, voter suppression or disenfranchisement in the southern states, denial of economic opportunity or resources nationwide, and private acts of violence and mass racial violence aimed at African Americans unhindered or encouraged by government authorities.

"The Supreme Court ruling regarding segregated schools essentially maintained that 'separate but equal' was satisfactory," advised Joyce. "That sounds okay, doesn't it? What could be unfair, Eddie?"

Eddie shrugged, then, suggested, "The blacks didn't like it because they wanted to be in and around whites?"

"Just deserved to die, be killed?"

Eddie did not respond.

"Here, Eddie is what the real problem was. 'Separate But Equal' was a lie. The black schools never were funded so as to provide facilities and educations equal to those of the white ones."

"What did they do, could they do?" asked Eddie.

"It's what's next from Wikipedia," Joy responded and then continued reading.

Great Migration and Civil Rights Movement

An African-American boy outside of Cincinnati, Ohio in the 1940s.

The desperate conditions of African Americans in the South that sparked the Great Migration of the early 20th century, combined with a growing African-American community in the Northern United States, led to a movement to fight violence and discrimination against African Americans that, like abolitionism before it, crossed racial lines. The Civil Rights Movement from 1954 to 1968 was directed at abolishing racial discrimination against African Americans, particularly in the Southern United States.

The March on Washington for Jobs and Freedom and the conditions which brought it into being are credited with putting pressure on President John F. Kennedy and Lyndon B. Johnson.

Via Wikipedia

View from the Lincoln Memorial toward the Washington Monument on August 28, 1963 (Wikipedia)

"Ever hear of Martin Luther King, Eddie?" asked Joyce.

"On some street signs?"

"Very good but that was not true on August 28, 1963, when he led the civil rights march on Washington. It was, however, the day on which he delivered his unforgettable 'I Have A Dream' speech.

Here, is an excerpt from it, Eddie," she said as she gave him an additional document, "Please read it aloud."

Let us not wallow in the valley of despair, I say to you today, my friends.

And so even though we face the difficulties of today and tomorrow, I still have a dream. It is a dream deeply rooted in the American dream.

I have a dream that one day this nation will rise and live out the true meaning of its creed: "We hold these truths to be self-evident, that all men are created equal."

I have a dream that one day on the red hills of Georgia, the sons of former slaves and the sons of former slave owners will be able to sit down together at the table of brotherhood.

I have a dream that one day even the state of Mississippi, a state sweltering with the heat of injustice, sweltering with the heat of oppression, will be transformed into an oasis of freedom and justice.

I have a dream that my four little children will one day live in a nation where they will not be judged by the color of their skin but by the content of their character.

I have a dream today!

I have a dream that one day, down in Alabama, with its vicious racists, with its governor having his lips dripping with the words of "interposition" and "nullification" -- one day right there in Alabama little black boys and black girls will be able to join hands with little white boys and white girls as sisters and brothers.

I have a dream today!

I have a dream that one day every valley shall be exalted, and every hill and mountain shall be made low, the rough places will be made plain, and the crooked places will be made straight; "and the glory of the Lord shall be revealed, and all flesh shall see it together."

"Nice reading Eddie," congratulated Joy.

Eddie smiled and admitted, "I got caught up in it, Joy."

"Alright," and Joyce went on with, more of the Wikipedia print out,"

Johnson put his support behind passage of the Civil Rights Act of 1964 that banned discrimination in public accommodations, employment, and labor unions, and the Voting Rights Act of 1965, which expanded federal authority over states to ensure black political participation through protection of voter registration and elections. By 1966, the emergence of the Black Power movement, which lasted from 1966 to 1975, expanded upon the aims of the Civil Rights Movement to include economic and political self-sufficiency, and freedom from white authority.

"Circumstances likely to improve greatly for Blacks, Eddie? Maybe in the direction of taking jobs away from whites in a big way?"

"I don't have any facts, but, yes, I would guess it would be trouble for whites."

"Okay, I'll continue with the facts," Joyce advised.

From 1965 to 1969, black family income rose from 54 to 60 percent of white family income. In 1968, 23 percent of black families earned under $3,000 a year, compared with 41 percent in 1960. In 1965, 19 percent of black Americans had incomes equal to the national median, a proportion that rose to 27 percent by 1967. In 1960, the median level of education for blacks had been 10.8 years, and by the late Sixties, the figure rose to 12.2 years, half a year behind the median for white.

"What do you think, Eddie?" Joyce wanted to know.

"Well, they weren't up with whites but made significant progress."

"Like anyone would do – better themselves, right Eddie?

"Well, well, yes." Eddie realized he had drawn himself into no win situation and went quiet.

Joyce did not press it.

Chapter 9 – US History & More

Sunday, October 9, 2016, Home of Joyce Levinson, 1:00 PM

Having gotten a late morning start, Joyce slipped lunch to about one o'clock. She rustled up some left-overs which Eddie once again lauded. Then they resumed in the living room.

Joyce opened. "Going forward I will not lose sight of our goal to understand what is going on locally. That would be Portland and Oregon. Yes?"

"Yes," agreed Eddie.

"However," Joyce continued, "I believe we must also be able to appreciate what is happening in our country and this may be the best time to dwell on the big picture. Yes?"

"Yes," agreed, Eddie once again.

"Good," Joyce responded. With all this settled I will begin by sharing with you the *Demography of the United States* from Wikipedia. She gave Eddie a copy and then began reading:

Demography of the United States

As of October 15, 2016, the United States has a total resident population of 324,707,000, making it the third most populous country in the world. It is very urbanized, with 81% residing in cities and suburbs as of 2014 (the worldwide urban rate is 54%). California and Texas are the most populous states as the mean center of U.S. population consistently shifts westward, and southward. New York City is the most populous US city.

Joyce paused to allow Eddie to digest the statistics and let him speak which after a short delay he did. "I had no idea about us being third most populous in the world and the concentration, 81% in cities. I'm not surprised that New York City is the biggest. Perhaps if I am lucky, I'll be able to visit there some day."

"Well, Eddie, "it would be my pleasure to visit New York City with you if you wouldn't mind traveling with an old lady."

"I wouldn't," Eddie immediately responded without thinking.

Frederic was suddenly on both their minds, but neither went there. Joyce continued with information from Wikipedia.

There were about 125.9 million adult women in the United States in 2014. The number of men was 119.4 million. At age 85 and older, there were almost twice as many women as men (4 million vs. 2.1 million). People under 21 years of age made up over a quarter of the U.S. population (27.1%), and people age 65 and over made up one-seventh (14.5%). The national median age was 36.8 years in 2009.

The United States Census Bureau defines White people as those "having origins in any of the original peoples of Europe, the Middle East, or North Africa. It includes people who reported "White" or wrote in entries such as

Irish, German, Italian, Lebanese, Near Easterner, Arab, or Polish." Whites constitute the majority of the U.S. population, with a total of about 245,532,000 or 77.7% of the population as of 2013. 62.6% of the population of the country are not-Hispanic whites. Despite major changes due to immigration since the 1960s, and the higher birth-rates of nonwhites, the current overall majority of American citizens are still white, and English-speaking, though regional differences exist.

"So," Joyce stopped to summarize, "while there are all of these minorities hate movements on the increase, *'The current overall majority of American citizens are still white, and English-speaking.'*

"Yes," agreed, Eddie, "but, that doesn't mean there are no pressures and competitions."

"True, Eddie, but it would be helpful to remember that we are a nation of immigrants. Yes?"

Eddie felt trapped but finally, gave in. Joy continued.

The American population almost quadrupled during the 20th century—at a growth rate of about 1.3% a year—from about 76 million in 1900 to 281 million in 2000. It reached the 200 million mark in 1968, and the 300 million mark on October 17, 2006. Population growth is fastest among minorities as a whole, and according to the Census Bureau's estimation for 2012, 50.4% of American children under the age of 1 belonged to minority groups.

Hispanic and Latino Americans accounted for 48% of the national population growth of 2.9 million between July 1, 2005, and July 1, 2006. Immigrants and their U.S.-born descendants are expected to provide most of the U.S. population gains in the decades ahead.

"You see?" commented Eddie. "Let's focus more on Portland and Oregon and maybe the Northwest."

"I agree, and I have much in that direction to share with you. However, why don't we take a break and stroll outside for a bit."

"Sounds good to me, Joyce," Eddie replied.

They walked towards the center of the city and before they knew it were fronting the Pioneer Courthouse Square and looking out at the Courthouse.

On the other side of the Courthouse, they came upon for what they were looking, Pioneer Place mall.

In the far corner from the open atrium, they found a neat little restaurant. It was getting on towards late afternoon, and they settled down to have dinner there.

After a while, Joyce brought out a notebook and suggested, that for a change, they could proceed with their project right there. Eddie liked the idea, and Joyce handed him a copy of a website printout titled, "GENTRIFICATION SPOTLIGHT: How Portland is Pushing Out Its Black Residents." It was dated April 18, 2016. She was about to dive into the article as she gazed around the room at several people happily dining with their children. It struck her hard, and she asked, "Eddie when was the last time you saw or spoke with your mother or sister?"

Eddie was taken back by the unexpected question and looked with raised eyebrows at Joyce. Finally, he responded, "Somewhere around five years ago when I hit

116

Morris with the frypan and ran away. Why are you asking me about it now?"

"I'll tell you in a minute. First tell me where you were all living?"

"In, in," stammered Eddie, "Hillsboro, but so what?"

"Don't you ever wonder about them and whether they wonder about you?"

Eddie's eyes began to water, and his upset was obvious. "Yes," he finally responded, "but with Morris and all what could I do?"

"Maybe call your mother... what's her name?"

"Mildred, Millie... Rawlins. She never took Morris's last name."

"Don't you think it would be a good idea to call her and let her and your sister know that you are okay?"

"But Joyce," Eddie began, "But, but..."

"I'm going to a search on my cell phone for Mildred Rawlins. If I find a current number, the rest will be up to you."

"Please, Joyce can't we just go on with the Portland history."

"After I try to find a contact number for your mother. Try to relax. Nothing terrible is going to happen. I'm just going to search for her number. Take a deep breath and go easy on yourself."

After a few minutes, Joyce asked, "Does Baldwin Drive sound right?"

Eddie, breathing heavily, nodded.

"How about calling her?"

Eddie shook his head vigorously.

"How about letting me call her... just to let her know you are alright?"

Eddie exhaled and finally said, "Just don't tell her where I am."

Joyce dialed the number and then put the phone on speaker.

"Hello, this is Millie," responded Eddie's mother.

"Millie, my name is Joyce, and I am a friend of your son, Eddie."

"Oh my God! Tell me he's alright, that nothing bad has happened to him."

"He's okay physically. In good shape."

"Is he there with you now? May I hear his voice?"

Joyce remained silent but nodded to Eddie.

"Ma," he finally responded, "I'm okay, I love you. Tell me you and Audrey are okay."

"Oh, Eddie, Eddie. We're getting by, but I feel so bad about what happened to you. It was all my fault. Should never have allowed Morris to treat you so badly. Please don't hate me."

"You shouldn't tell Morris that we talked."

"Tell him? Tell him? No way. He's long gone and good riddance. I couldn't abide him after I had lost you and Morris finally left. Please tell me you'll let me see you again."

Eddie went quiet, and after a while, Joyce spoke, "This is Joyce, Millie. I will help Eddie to work out a way to visit with you, and I promise that we'll call again in a few days."

"I love you, Eddie," were Millies last words as the call ended.

"Eddie, there are those who will deny Portland's history as presented in this document. However, you only need to do a Google search on something like 'Portland Oregon white supremacist history,' and you'll be shocked at the coverage. This 'GENTRIFICATION SPOTLIGHT' article is one that is representative in the information it presents. It tells of actual difficulties people had in finding Portland lodgings. Please read from it."

Eddie began:

Between its alarming legacy of racism and its skyrocketing rents, Portland, Oregon, has become one and gentrification. What will it take for this hipster heartland to live up to its warm and fuzzy reputation?

Update on 4-20-16: Portland native Marih Alyn-Claire has notified Colorlines that, after months of searching, she found an affordable apartment in the city.

Marih Alyn-Claire, a Black 64-year-old Portland, Oregon, native, is afraid she will soon be homeless. Last summer, she learned that her rent would rise by several hundred dollars in June 2016, but so far she hasn't found a decent apartment that she can afford. "I've watched the redlining here. I've lived through discrimination myself," she said at an emergency housing forum with state representatives and senators in January. "But I've always been able to get a place."

Until now.

Alyn-Claire lives on Social Security Disability insurance and pays for part of her housing costs with a federal

*Section 8 voucher. In recent years, though, Portland
rents have skyrocketed, and the federal government's
voucher program hasn't kept pace - leaving tenants like
her to shoulder the cost or meet the streets.*

*There is no one story of displacement in Portland. Among
the 30 others who testified at the January emergency
housing hearing was a working-class mother pushed out,
a copywriter evicted and grappling with doubled rent
costs, and a domestic violence service provider having
trouble finding emergency housing for clients.*

Eddie suddenly stopped reading. "Joyce," he began,
"I want to see my mother… and sister."

"That's a very good idea," approved Joyce, "and this
is a good place to break off from the article. Let's head
on home. We can talk along the way and later on I'll
whip up something for dinner."

"I appreciate your patience and kindness, Joyce"
Eddie revealed honestly. He was, however, still very
torn. *How am I going to be able to kill you?* Eddie
pondered. *Frederic will surely help me or maybe he'll
change his mind. Whatever happens, I have to do what's
right.* Eddie then gave himself over to figuring out how to
visit with his mother and Audrey.

Chapter 10 – Mildred & Audrey

Sunday, Oct. 9, 2016, On Way to Joy's Home, 5:00 PM

"How shall we do this, Joyce?" Eddie asked.

"By calling again and asking if, when and where your mother would want to meet with you, us."

"Yes, yes, let's call her back right now, please Joyce."

"Shall I suggest tomorrow, Columbus day, Eddie? At my house?"

"Yes, Columbus Day, yes, yes," Eddie responded while jumping up and down.

"Shh here goes."

"Millie, this Joyce again. Okay if I call you Millie. Wonderful and you can call me Joy if you wish. Goodness, no. I'm old enough to be Eddie's grandmother. Eddie's with me still, and I'm going to put the phone on speaker. How's that?"

"Excellent," replied Mildred."

"Hi Ma, I want to see you," Eddie shouted out. "Tomorrow on Columbus Day. Audrey too."

"I am more than ready, son."

"Me too!" Audrey yelled.

"I live near downtown Portland," advised Joyce, " not far from a Tri-Met MAX light rail stop, and you're welcome to visit at my home."

"I don't know who you are Joyce, but you are truly a Joy. Just give me the directions and time, and we'll be there."

"We'll do better than that, Millie. One or both of us will meet you at the stop."

"I'll be there," shouted Eddie. "Come early."

"Is 10 AM too early?" Millie wanted to know.

"No," responded Joyce and she proceeded to advise the stop to get off. "Until tomorrow." she finished.

"Tomorrow!" Eddie shouted.

Joyce could not remember the last time she experienced such happiness as that which filled her as she witnessed Eddie's pleasure in all that had taken place.

They arrived at Joyce's home near 5:30 and Joyce, true to her word, whipped up a decent meal quickly from leftovers. Then she informed Eddie, "Into the living room we have work to do.

Eddie picked up with reading where he left off with the "GENTRIFICATION SPOTLIGHT" article.

Despite what's happening, Portland is not known as an expensive city. Rather, it is seen as a haven for creatives and nonconformists, the place that popular comedy "Portlandia" famously deemed "the city where young people go to retire." The New York Times encourages tourists to "ignore the hype, and indulge the city's simple pleasures—from $4 films to puppet museum" or enjoy "shockingly affordable" delicious eats. Portland is fast becoming accessible only to the wealthiest iconoclasts. Since 2010, rents have increased *an average of 20 percent, sixth-fastest rise in the nation after cities like New York and San Jose. In 2015, Portland ranked first in the country percentage of land tracts identified as gentrifying by Governing Magazine.*

With rent hikes of more than 15 percent in the third quarter of 2015, tenant organizations began calling the months of July and August "the summer of evictions." There's been a vast increase in the number of single-person households living in Central City, the urban core—often college graduates attracted by Portland's relative affordability and hip reputation. And thanks to state laws that prohibit policies used to regulate other pricey cities, Portland tenants are vulnerable to limitless rent increases.

"Summer of evictions…limitless rent increases." Joyce quoted. "It's why New York and other cities have rent control legislation. Is this not terrible, Eddie?"

Eddie shrugged and asked if he should continue reading. Joyce stifled her upset and nodded for him to continue.

New White Majorities in Traditionally Black Neighborhoods

The media has paid a lot of attention to the White artists affected by the rent crisis, the "urban pioneers" ditching Portland in search of greater affordability and a more authentic cultural scene. But Portland's people of color—and particularly, Black residents—have been hardest hit.

While White Portland has more than rebounded since the last recession, poverty in the Black community has worsened. From 2000 to 2013, White incomes grew from about $55,000 to $60,000; Black incomes fell from $35,000 to less than $30,000. A report published last April by the Portland Housing Bureau revealed there is not a single neighborhood in the city where an average African-American can afford a two-bedroom apartment.

Black Portlanders suffer enormously from this catastrophic combination of falling incomes and rising housing costs. In 2015, the number of Black homeless people grew by 48 percent. *Though they make up only 7 percent of Portland residents, Black people constitute a disproportionate 25 percent of the homeless population.*

While the entire city is facing the stress of rising rents, Portland's Black community has grappled with gentrification for more than a decade. From 2000 to 2010, the city's core lost 10,000 Black residents. In the historically Black neighborhoods of the Northeast such as King, Woodlawn, and Boise-Eliot, Whites became the new majority in most census tracts.

"This is a critical moment for us as a state ... as we're faced with quite possibly the most far-reaching and devastating housing crisis in Oregon's history due to unprecedented rent increases," Katrina Holland, deputy director of the Community Alliance of Tenants, said at the January hearing with politicians. The crisis, she said, ravages "people who look like me, African-American, and Native Americans, on top of generations of racially motivated, dramatic displacements."

"Have you not yourself suffered some of these difficulties, Eddie?" asked Joyce.

"Yes," he answered without further comment.

"And you're not even black. Does it somehow seem unreasonable to blame this on blacks and other people of color? Well, Eddie?"

"It doesn't seem right," he finally acknowledged. *Maybe Frederic will have some answers,* he pondered, beginning to feel he was between a rock and a hard place.

Joyce did not press him and moved forward with reading herself.

The Racial Failure of 'New Urbanism.'

The housing crunch Portland is suffering is happening in cities across the country. White millennials, eager to live close to where they work and access the cultural vibrancy of city life, are driving up demand for housing and displace Black and Latino residents from the neighborhoods they helped to build. One study of 11 metropolitan areas found that from 2000 to 2010 there was an increase in the Black population living outside the urban core in each city. While some Black homeowners may sell their houses and leave the city for better opportunities, tenants are often unable to afford to live in rejuvenated neighborhoods. Other Black homeowners are bought out by eager investors, only to find that they are unable to rent or purchase housing elsewhere.

Portland, already abnormally White due to a history of racial exclusion and forced removal of Black residents, is a dramatic example of a nationwide problem.

With its municipal compost system and bike-friendly streets, Portland is a model for the nation of "new urbanism"—a vision of thriving neighborhoods with low carbon footprints. Some say that the city has failed to invest sufficiently in the livelihoods of Black residents, depriving them of the opportunity to enjoy recent public investments in the landscape.

"If Portland is trying to be this model of sustainable, livable, walkable, 20-minute cities, and it's not racially diverse, and it's not class diverse, we've got big problems about what that means for anywhere else," says Lisa Bates, a professor of urban planning at Portland State University. "Is it only viable to use public resources to create a favorable environment if you get rid of all the undesirable people?"

Portland officials say they value class and racial diversity and are making efforts to address the larger city crisis. Last October, the city, along with Los Angeles, Seattle and the state of Hawaii, declared a housing and homeless state of emergency, enacting measures to open new shelters, legalize homeless encampments and set aside funding for affordable housing. In Portland, the ordinance allowed the city to broaden its current focus on homeless veterans to the city's growing number of women and families with no place to live. Affordable housing advocates recognize the declaration as a step toward addressing the rent crisis.

Will Portland get to the roots of housing displacement in Portland's Black community—roots that run deep, that go back centuries?

"Let's stop here for today. Tomorrow after your Mother's and Audrey's visit, we'll pick up with your reading of 'Jim Crow, Portland Style,'" suggested Joyce. "Anything else before the big meeting tomorrow, Eddie?"

"No, going to bed. I'm beat out."

"Me too," advised Joyce, "a difficult Portland history day but a good day otherwise."

"Yes, a good day and, 10 o'clock tomorrow will be even better. Thank you for everything today, Joyce."

"Rest well, buddy," Joyce finished.

Monday, Oct. 10, 2016, Tri-Met MAX Stop, Nearby Joyce's House, 10 AM.

"Try to stop fidgeting, Eddie," Joyce requested.

"I'll try," responded Eddie, not wanting to argue with her just as the train pulled in.

"Eddie!" shouted out Millie as she stepped off.

They hugged each other for a long time and both cried.

"I guess I don't count," complained Audrey.

She took up a position next to Joyce.

"Come on here," Joyce responded as she turned to the young woman, offering a warm hug.

"I like you," Audrey mumbled, "you're nice."

"So are you," answered Joyce while planting a kiss on the girl's forehead.

Audrey walked with Joyce as she led them back to her house. Eddie and his mother followed arm in arm behind them.

On arriving at the house, Joyce took up her usual armchair seat with Eddie on the sofa between his sister and his mother.

Millie looked around and marveled that at her good fortune. "I apologize, Eddie, for failing you with Morris and all. I will do anything to make it up to you. Do you want to come home to Hillsboro with us?"

Joyce waited silently to hear Eddie's reply.

"I can't do that right now, Ma. Joyce and I are working on something right now, and she lets me use her guest room."

Audrey raised her eyebrows in wonderment about which Eddie could be talking.

"I don't understand, Eddie," Millie complained.

"Tell her," ordered Joyce, "or I will."

"I have a good friend, the name of Frederic. He was there for me when I was alone and had no one."

Joyce offered a small box of tissues to Millie who was struggling not to interrupt her son's explanation as painful as it was.

"And Joyce," puzzled Audrey, as she looked to both Eddie and Joyce for an explanation.

Eddie decided to take the initiative, fearing what Joyce might reveal. "You see," Eddie began, "Frederic heads up this organization that is against people they think is a problem… not that they have a history of harming anyone. And, it's probably an error, but they identified Joyce as a possible problem and asked me to investigate."

"And Frederic is still your friend and Joyce is allowing you to use her guest room. None of it makes sense. Audrey?" appealed Millie to her daughter.

"I also don't get it," she responded.

Joyce remained silent to allow Eddie every opportunity to work through this. However, when it became clear that he was stuck, she decided to intervene.

"For what it's worth I'll tell everything I know." She started by looking at Eddie who winced and looked scared.

"Eddie was, is, under orders from Frederic who heads up the Oregon Feistys, a white supremacist organization. To date, they have not manifested themselves in any real way except to recruit vulnerable young men like Eddie."

"Did they give you a weapon, Eddie?" his mother wanted to know."

On discerning that Eddie wasn't able to answer, Joyce stepped in once again. "I have the gun they gave to Eddie under lock and key in a safe in my bedroom," advised Joyce."

By this time it was clear there was no hiding anything, and Eddie decided to make the best case for his tie in with Frederic and the Feistys and, of course, Joyce. "You have to understand that Frederic feels that certain elements in our society are not good for us, people of color and also especially Jews. I don't think they will hurt anyone, they probably just want them gone."

"And that's why they gave you a gun?" Millie questioned. "And how do you get involved with all this, Joyce?" Millie added.

Stymied again and silent, Joyce resumed. "My last name, the name of my demised husband, John, is Levinson."

"Are you Jewish," asked Audrey.

"No, but they think I am and put Eddie onto keeping a watch on me. I found out about this and decided that I could report Eddie to the police which might not have done any good or that I could try to save Eddie from making a terrible mistake. I may be a fool, but I'm 61 years old with no children or grandchildren. So what did I have to lose?"

"Joyce, you made a deal with Eddie?" asked his mother.

"I did. I made Eddie give me his gun and made Eddie agree to listen to me about everything I learned over the years, starting with Hitler. Also the results of my research into Neo-Nazism, SkinHeads, White Supremacy and other hate organizations whatever the names."

"And he has been cooperating with you?" Millie wanted to know.

"Yes," responded Joyce, "but he still stays in touch with Frederic, which I accept is necessary for him right now."

"How far have you come in your education, Joyce," Audrey asked.

"A long way. We're now well into the Northwest and what is going on in Portland and Oregon that is shocking."

"Please let me sit in," begged Audrey, "I can arrange some time off from school with no problem."

"Me too, I want in too," Millie pleaded. "I'll find a place somehow for Audrey and myself to stay."

"How would a pull-out sleeping two be for you?"

"Fine," responded Millie.

"Yeah," Audrey agreed.

"Good, you're sitting on it," advised Joyce. "What say, Eddie?"

"Do I have a choice?" he asked.

"No," answered Joyce, "but you might want to update Frederic. Tell him they're my relatives if you want, but not Levinson." Turning one by one to Millie, Audrey and finally, Eddie, she added, "We'll remember this as one heck of a Columbus Day. Thank you, Christopher."

Chapter 11 Portland

Tues., Oct. 11, 2016, Joyce Levinson's House, 9:00 AM.

Eddie and Joyce were in the living room and preparing to dive into where they last left off when the door bell ring. "Could that be Millie and Audrey? No, it's way too early," responded Joyce. "We better see who it is," she said as she went to the door with Eddie following close behind.

"Millie, Audrey, you're here already!" Joyce exclaimed. "Set your bags down over by the sofa. We'll find a place later where you can unpack. Eddie and I were just getting ready to resume where we last left off about Portland."

"Let's do it," said Millie setting herself down at one end of the couch. She patted the space next to her and motioned for Audrey to sit there.

"Okay," acknowledged a surprised Joyce. "Sit down next to Audrey, Eddie, and we'll begin where we left off. Read, please."

Eddie picked up the printout from the coffee table and began.

Jim Crow, Portland Style

Michelle Lewis, a therapist with connections to Black residents throughout Portland, can see the links between the city's history of racial exclusion, her clients' housing instability, and her hardship. Since she and her husband lost their home to predatory lending during the recession, she says, they have been forced to move five times—most recently, beyond the city limits—as a result of rent increases and racial discrimination.

"We've felt like nomads," she says.

Oregon's first Black residents may have felt similarly. In the 1840s, the territory passed laws prohibiting Blacks from living in the state and punishing those who tried to remain with whiplashes and expulsion. In 1858, Oregon became the only state in the country admitted with a clause in its constitution excluding Blacks. As a result, Oregon's Black population grew slowly—and those who stayed navigated Jim Crow-style segregation.

Lewis' grandfather came to Portland during World War II. During that time, the Kaiser Company imported thousands of Whites and Blacks from across the country to build tanks and cargo ships. White Portlanders, averse to the growing Black population, confined most of the migrants to a new development called Vanport, built on a flood plane by the Columbia River.

"That's where we had to live at," Lewis recalls her grandparents explaining. "If you worked downtown, you had to be over in that area by a certain time, or else you could be fined, you could be jailed." (While there is no official record of the so-called "sundown laws" in Oregon, there is a rich oral history detailing how towns jailed Black people for appearing after dark, especially in southern Oregon.)

134

Millie's and Audrey's astonishment at what Eddie's reading revealed was evident by the looks on their faces.

Eddie paused briefly to allow them the opportunity to comment and then continued.

After the war, Portland residents wanted Vanport gone, and developers wanted the property for parkland and manufacturing use. In 1948, they got their wishes: After city officials had failed to warn residents of rising river levels, dikes broke, flooding Vanport and killing 13 people. Lewis' family lost their home in the flood.

Eddie showed them a picture of a mural commemorating the event. He waited as they passed it around.

Photo: Abigail Savitch-Lew

"13 dead, terrible," assessed Millie.
"Awful," Audrey added, revealing her upset.
"Yes," Joyce agreed.
Eddie continued reading.

Like many other Black residents of Vanport, the Lewis family settled in the Albina neighborhood of the Northeast, one of the only areas of the city where realtors would sell to Blacks. As White residents fled to the suburbs, banks redlined the neighborhood, depriving Black tenants of the opportunity to obtain mortgages and build home equity, while investors purchased homes with cash and let them sit empty. With the city turning a blind eye and rising poverty, crime and unemployment, White Portlanders began to view Albina as a dangerous slum.

When Lewis looks back on her childhood in Albina, she remembers a close-knit community and good times spent on friends' porches, climbing fruit trees and playing four-corner kickball. "We would play outside all day 'til the streetlights came on," she recalls. "You could go and knock on your neighbor's door—my mom would say, go and knock Mrs. Shirley's [door], I need an egg. ... You knew everybody in the neighborhood."

Instead of nurturing this community, the Portland Development Commission launched numerous "urban renewal" projects with the purported goal of addressing blight. Aiming to convert the land to commercial and industrial uses, the city displaced hundreds of residents to build a sports arena, expand a hospital, and construct two new highways.

By the 1970s, public outcry against "urban renewal" caused officials to change course: The city let the area remain residential and supported local initiatives to revitalize housing and streetscapes. Black Portlanders were still shut out. White people with higher incomes returned to the Northend, causing rents to rise and uprooting many Black businesses and about one in every four Black residents.

With the loss of many members of this community has come the loss of history, leading to the false perception that Portland is naturally White, or that uncontrollable market forces bear sole responsibility for the displacement. For Lewis, the erasure is painful.

"Naturally White! What a joke!" Joyce could hardly control herself. Started to cry. Eddie got up and walked around to where she was sitting. He stroked her neck and back. Joyce reached up and squeezed his hand.

Millie and Audrey watched silently, somewhat puzzled.

"Read, Eddie, from where I left off with Lewis," Joyce requested at last.

"It's a horrible feeling, to come to a neighborhood where you grow up in, and have the people there look at you as if you don't belong," she says. She recalls Little Chapel of the Chimes, the funeral home where she buried her grandfather. Little Chapel of the Chimes is now a craft beer pub.

Oregon imprisons African Americans at a higher rate than most other states

June 30, 2014. Oregon imprisons African Americans at a rate higher than most other states; a new report revealed this week.

For every 1,000 black residents, about 21 are in prison, the seventh-highest rate in the country. Oregon's rate is nearly double Washington's and 46 percent higher than the national average.

The study from the national nonprofit Sentencing Project mined data from the U.S. Census and the U.S. Bureau of Justice Statistics. It found African Americans make up more than 9 percent of Oregon's prison population, though they comprise only 1.8 percent of the state's general population. One of every 21 black men in Oregon is in prison.

The report follows an unrelated February study that found black people overrepresented in every aspect of Multnomah County's criminal justice system. Both studies confirm what communities of color have known for a long time, said Bobbin Singh, executive director of the Oregon Justice Resource Center.

"It's horrifying," Singh said. "As Oregonians, we should be embarrassed by this and working hard to transform our criminal justice system so that it's fair and transparent. When you have racial disparities that exist at both the county and state level, the perception of our criminal justice system is it's discriminatory. And if you have a discriminatory justice system, it's not going to be perceived as credible."

*There's no clear reason why Oregon has such a high
rate, Singh said. Socioeconomic issues and implicit and
explicit racial bias likely all contribute.*

"First chance I have I'm moving out of here,"
declared Audrey.

Having lost Eddie for so many years, the thought of
losing Audrey was more than Millie could accept. "I'll
go with you Audrey if you'll let me."

"Of course, Ma," responded Audrey.

"Don't count Eddie out," put in Joyce "and don't
jump into something before we finish here. We have
much more to cover."

All of this was doing a number on Eddie who was
still pondering his relationship with Frederic. He was
happy when Joyce pressed, "Read more, Eddie."

*The Multnomah County study, part of the MacArthur
Foundation's National Safety & Justice Challenge,
suggested blacks face discrimination in every aspect of
the criminal justice system — from when they're first
stopped all the way through their time in court.*

*That report found that blacks in Multnomah County are
4.2 times more likely to be referred to the district
attorney's office for a case review and 4.1 times more
likely to have a case accepted for prosecution. While
blacks make up only 5 percent of the county's
population overall, they represent 27 percent of its jail
population.*

*Together, the reports "should spark outrage and a
sense of urgency among elected leaders," said David
Rogers, the executive director of the American Civil
Liberties Union of Oregon.*

"I'm a little afraid that people may become desensitized to the disturbing news of institutional racism in the criminal justice system," Rogers said. "I'm left to wonder, are we doomed to continue the cycle? All the data in the world won't fix a lack of political will. We need more of that — in a bad way."

"Eddie, is your friend Frederic going to fix any of this?" Millie wanted to know.

"I'm not sure, maybe," he lied.

"You need, to be honest about this, Eddie," challenged Joyce, "especially with yourself."

Millie decided not to pursue the issue at this point. "Please continue reading, Eddie." she prompted.

Multnomah County received a $150,000 grant last year from the MacArthur Foundation to create a fairer jail system.

Tackling the problem statewide will take a widespread approach, reform advocates said.

Studies like the one from the Sentencing Project are good for instigating conversations, advocates said. But they also say they need more information to understand what leads African Americans to prison in the first place.

State lawmakers, Singh said, should require every major Oregon county to match Multnomah County's analysis of its criminal justice system. Rogers said police agencies across the state should follow Portland's lead and publish data about the race of the people officers stop.

And both said district attorneys and their offices need to become more transparent.

"I had no idea," revealed Millie, "this is terrible."
"So maybe we'll leave sooner," assessed Audrey.
Joyce did not comment.
Eddie decided it was time to get back to the reading even though he well understood his mother's and sister's concerns.

"The district attorney is the most powerful actor in our system," Singh said. "They decide whether to charge someone with a crime and those charges are, to dismiss a case, to negotiate a plea or go to trial. That's where we need to focus our attention. It's an elected position, so we can ask district attorneys to implement policies to help drive down disparities."

In Multnomah County, District Attorney Rod Underhill said his office is trying several approaches.

After the February report, Underhill instituted mandatory, annual equity and diversity training for his staff. His attorneys also have attended continuing education classes on implicit bias and equity.

"Will that help my deputies to be more aware? I sure hope so. I want to be better," Underhill said. "But this isn't a one-off, you do this, and you're done. You have to be creative."

Earlier this month, he announced his office would no longer automatically prosecute teenagers in adult court for some Measure 11 crimes.

"What a mess," commented Millie.
"It is," supported Joyce.

Audrey just smiled, and Eddie continued reading.

Underhill is also helping start a $1 million county-funded program that will send drug users to treatment rather than jail. A similar program in Seattle found that blacks were disproportionately arrested downtown for drug-use and prostitution offenses.

"We're going to divert them before they ever go to jail," Underhill said. "When we send fewer people to prison, we're going to send fewer people of color to prison."

Statewide, Oregon has one tool, advocates said, that could help. In 2013, lawmakers gave themselves the power to ask for "racial impact" reports showing how proposed legislation and ballot measures might affect people of color.

"Talk, talk, talk," observed Audrey.

"Audrey, please," Millie began to admonish.

"No, Millie," Joyce interjected. She is right. I'll read on for a while, and you'll see how much needs doing." She looked to Eddie who nodded his agreement for her to read.

Lawmakers have asked for the racial impact statements only four times, the state's senior research analyst said. Those bills concerned youth offenders and never made it out of committee.

What Oregon needs if it hopes to address the disparity, Rogers said, is a tool that examines how current laws are affecting people of color.

"It's about the system that's in place," Rogers said. "Fixing this problem will require more than looking

forward. It will require us to look back at existing laws, at the system that is driving the disparity."

Until then, Rogers said, each imprisonment creates a new cycle of problems not yet forecast in the report.

"They are more likely to have challenges getting a job," Rogers said. "They're going to have a harder time accessing education, housing and a range of services.

This disparity then creates the cycle of intergenerational poverty. Children of incarcerated parents are much less likely to finish school. They're going to have a lower family income. It's deep, deeply troubling." Casey Parks, Oregonian

Portland, Oregon Deemed "Most Racist" City In The United States, Posted three years earlier

In a recent nationwide survey conducted by the Oklahoma Symposium of Racial Studies, researchers claim to have pinpointed the individual US cities that are most plagued by racism. The list included locations such as Atlanta, GA, Phoenix, AZ and Chicago, IL. However, the city crowned most infected with the cancer of racial intolerance came as a shocker to many: The so-called "liberal" utopia of Portland OR.

"You can run away, Audrey, but you may find it difficult to locate a place that's clear of this. Perhaps will be better to work on Portland becoming the place we want it to be," advised Joyce. "Think about it?"

"I will if my mother and brother are up for that."

143

Eddie could not help but appreciate being part of a family again. "And Joyce, he demanded," while still wondering how to factor in Frederic.

Joyce continued reading.

Yes, it seems the City Of Roses came out at the top of the list for most racial tension, blowing all the other cities away with their tie-dyed, race-riot.

Researchers cite several instances in which the occupants engaged in activities which would make one think that underneath all the hipster attire lurks a horde of rabid Klansmen in hippie's clothing. From run-of-the-mill racism to even more abstract and subtle forms of prejudices that can only be found in the rainy, northwestern city, PDX seems to be brimming with bigotry.

On the heels of this study comes Portland's annual White Man March, organized by the white nationalist group, American Freedom Party. The North West chapter of ANIFA were helpless to stop the gathering, which took place Saturday, March 15th. In a shocking twist, most of ANTIFA's Portland members have succumbed to the racism that surrounds them and becomes remorseless fascists themselves.

"It just goes on and on," commented Millie. "Keep on reading Joyce."

Portland schools also employ racial segregation during their parent/teacher conferences. The superintendent of Portland's public school system declined to comment, but it's suspected that the reason behind the school's separation of parents by their skin color is to avoid any potential confrontations between racial groups. A teacher in the Parkrose district who wishes to remain anonymous told National Report the following.

"The African Americans are resentful of the whites because they have gentrified their old neighborhoods, pushing them further and further out towards the fringes of the city."

On the opposite end of this racial divide are the progressive liberals, whose heart's bleed for whatever cause is deemed most chic. They hate themselves for being white, yet think lowly enough of the African Americans to assume they always require their heroic assistance. Portland seems to be more of a lily-white utopia for haughty pseudo-humanitarians rather than the cornucopia of diversity that it is as commonly portrayed.

You will find the highest concentration of these closet-racists primarily in the heart of Portland. The city itself is ivory faces as far as the eye can see until you wander out away from the city that you will begin to see any other races intermingling with the sea of snowy white bodies. It is an unspoken truth that Portland is predominantly white, and they want to keep it that way.

Joyce could tell from Eddie's heavy breathing how much the reading affected him. She motioned to Mildred who pulled him close. Then he turned and looked up into Joyce's eyes and asked, "There's more to come isn't there?"

"Do you want to stop?"

"No, I want to know everything."

"I'm proud of you Eddie."

"We are both proud of you," added Millie.

"So am I," said Audrey refusing to be left out.

Eddie couldn't believe the abundance of praise. He never remembered anything like it before in his life.

Chapter 12 – US Nazism

Monday, October 10, 2016, Home of Joyce Levinson, 8:00 AM

They knocked on the door to the guest room. Then called out, "Ready or not, we're coming in, Eddie."

They could hear movement from within, and then, "Okay, come on in."

They opened the door to find Eddie sitting up in bed with the covers up almost to his chin. Portions of the tee shirt he was wearing escaped the concealment. "You need to get up," Audrey shouted as she jumped on the bed on top of his covers. "We have a lot to do."

"Isn't it nice to have a baby sister?" queried Joyce who stood at the end of the bed next to Millie.

"Our breakfasts are all set up and ready in the kitchen," his mother advised. "Were you planning on being served in bed?"

"No, Ma," a slightly embarrassed Eddie answered. "Please get off of me, Audrey."

"Okay, " she responded, "but you come out in a few minutes, or I'll be back, to drag you out. I' m stronger than I look."

With that said, the female trio exited the bedroom.

When Eddie arrived in the kitchen, one of Joy's deliciously prepared meals was already set out four times over, and he found something additional on his chair. "Pajamas!" he exclaimed.

"The pj's were John's," divulged Joyce. "Being the only man, err, young man, in a house, with three women, I decided you should have them, even though you'll probably find them a bit too big."

"I don't care. Beautiful pajamas, perfect."

"Shall we save breakfast until you put them on?" Audrey chuckled.

"No way, kiddo, but these are great," raved Eddie as he took his seat and began digging into the food ahead of the others. "What is everybody waiting for? " he asked. "We have a lot to do. What's up for today, Joyce?"

"Nazism in the United States," she advised as she began her meal. "Dig in everyone, enjoy."

Forty-five minutes later they were in the living room with Joyce in the armchair, and Eddie next to Audrey, next to Millie on the sofa.

Joyce began, "I don't know how much you know about the Feistys or Nazism in the United States, but I feel it's an important part of what is going on – I wish it to be less so, but we need to look at the reality of it. I'm going to begin reading from:

RISING NAZISM AND RACIAL INTOLERANCE IN THE UNITED STATES, A CONTEMPORARY ANALYSIS

"The document, dated April 30, 2015, is fairly much up to date. It is extensive, but for our needs, I think the introduction will be enough." She handed each of them a printout and began reading.

The historical circumstances regarding the emergence of Germanic Nazism in the 1920s were, in many ways, a product of long-held racial beliefs and undercurrents in German society. However, as Hannah Arendt points out, "Hitlerism exercised its strong international and inter-European appeal during the thirties because of racism, although a state doctrine only in Germany, had been a public trend in public opinion everywhere" (Arendt, 1966). Fascism in Europe predated Nazism. Mussolini's Italy, Franco's Spain, and other fascist states that emerged in Europe shared varying degrees of racial thinking; most placed less emphasis on theories of racial superiority in comparison to the Third Reich. In America, the Friends of New Germany, and later the German American Bund, emerged as pro-Nazi movements very much in keeping with Nazi Party in Germany, but with American cultural signifiers. (The Bund identified George Washington as the first real fascist.) The Bund was broken up during WW II, but a brand of American Nazism/white supremacy emerged in the post-years.

In 1959, the beginnings of a unique American culture of racism influenced by Nazism and fascism began to form. In that year, George Lincoln Rockwell inaugurated the American Nazi Party. A veteran with a commanding personality, Rockwell set down the principles that most modern neo-Nazi movements still follow: theories of racial purity that embrace essentially all European Americans; a virulent antiSemitism in keeping with traditional Nazism; and a fixation on a white supremacist version of Christianity (Simonelli, 1999). In the 1970s, neo-Nazi organizations began to meld with Ku Klux Klan groups. The Klan long represented America's best-known homegrown hate group, but with the rise of the Knights of the Ku Klux Klan and David Duke (himself a neo-Nazi), a new blended brand of hate organizing surfaced. In 1979, Klan groups and the American Nazi Party together murdered five anti-Klan activists in an event known as the "Greensboro Massacre." Duke's Klan elevated anti-Jewish conspiracies to the forefront in a way more in keeping with traditional Nazi/fascist organizations. Duke also helped usher in the era of the "sophisticated racist," one who could appeal to individuals who would never attend a racist gathering, but who embrace white supremacist/racist beliefs (ADL, 2013).

"The 'sophisticated racist,' what an idea?" commented Joyce. "Anything to draw people in." She waited for a response.

"I just can't figure out how people can eagerly get involved," Millie was the first to offer.

"Ignorance in a big way," offered Audrey.

Eddie shrugged, still dealing with Frederic promises.

Joy recognized he once again evaded a real answer and, in an attempt to get him more involved, asked him to pick up on the reading

Modern day racist intellectuals such as Jared Taylor of American Renaissance and John Derbyshire (formerly of National Review) represent the fruition of Duke's efforts to legitimize white supremacist thinking among the college educated. Along with Duke, a former physicist named William Pierce sought to establish an American version of a Nazi racial state by appealing to racists from all walks of life. (Zeskind, 2009) While Pierce sought "elite" members for membership in his organization, the National Alliance, he also penned novels like The Turner Diaries (a bestseller) and Hunter which appealed to lone and organized racists who dreamed of carrying out violent acts against minorities and even overthrowing the U.S. government. The men who bombed the Alfred P. Murrah Federal Building in 1995, Timothy McVeigh and Terry Nichols, both found with copies of Pierce's novels.

Joyce nearly gagged. "Pierce must have been very proud," she said.

Millie and Audrey nodded their agreement. Not expecting a meaningful response from Eddie, Joyce said, "It's okay Eddie. Continue reading."

The increasing melding of neo-Nazi, Ku Klux Klan and other white supremacist groups, also occurred in the prisons, influencing violent gangs like the Aryan Brotherhood. Neo-Nazis and other white supremacists have sought to join the U.S. military to familiarize themselves with weapons, training, and tactics in hopes they might be used back home in the event of a future "race war" (Kennard, 2012). While perhaps, most importantly, former Klansman Don Black used the power of the Internet and social media to create Stormfront, an online forum connecting racists around the world.

Joyce shook her head but did not otherwise interrupt his reading.

Though long removed from its native Germany, Nazism has morphed and combined with American white supremacist culture and organizations like the Ku Klux Klan. The power of the prison networks, literature, and now the Internet, are spreading the message of white racial supremacy across America and beyond. Thus, the

U.S. is one of the most important, perhaps the most important, the battlefield in the fight against the spread of contemporary racism. The psychological causes of individual's belief in racist, neo-Nazi, anti-Semitic, Islamophobic, and other hate-based ideologies are a complex question.

"Not if you just hate everyone who's not white or has wrong beliefs," Joy felt compelled to say. "Jews are always a problem," she observed.

"What a thing," commented Millie

Audrey shook her head in disbelief.

"Yes, Joyce," was as much as Eddie could muster. He, of course, knew something of where Frederic and the Feistys stood and until Joyce, felt he fit right in. He was relieved when Joyce said she'd pick up with the reading.

Many factors contribute to bringing someone to adopt these outlooks, and then to join organized groups based on them. Perhaps the most significant factor, or set of factors, in helping to dispose persons to take up such ideologies is economic disenfranchisement. There are many aspects to the experience of economic disenfranchisement, and each has specific kinds of consequences. Regarding predicting which individuals are most likely to join hate groups, social scientists have routinely identified low-income as the main driver. Low incomes drive some interrelated problems that can contribute to creating an environment which disposes of persons, especially young persons, to joining hate groups. The despair born of poverty and economic exclusion has long been known disproportionately to incentivize persons to acts of crime.

When faced with impoverished and degrading circumstances individuals often seek to rationalize this experience. Those with low incomes, who also tend to be disproportionately less well educated and have unequal access to social services and resources, are more susceptible to racist ideologies, and their claims other groups are to blame for the sufferings and privations experienced. In a society of increasing inequality and decreasing social mobility, many working families are caught in a trap of having to work harder and harder only to fall behind still, just more or less slowly.

"Can you identify with any of this, Eddie?" Joyce asked. She did not expect him to admit what was abundantly clear and he did not disappoint.

"I'm not sure," he lied.

Millie and Audrey more and more realized the awful perversion he was suffering

Well, my friend, Joyce thought, *we have limited time left to figure this out. I hope this doesn't end badly for all of us.* She continued the reading.

The great furor unleashed in the U.S. upon publication of Thomas Piketty's book in 2014 testifies to the widespread perception that inequality is at a new zenith, while mobility a new nadir. The research results contained therein confirm the veracity of this perception. Competition for increasingly fewer jobs, especially well-paying jobs continues to lead, as it has in the past, to racial tensions.

One recent research study in the U.S. from 2013 showed a clear link between the incidence of hate crimes and unemployment (Curthoys, 2013). Unemployment is only one phenomenon among a constellation of related economic tribulations faced by working class individuals and families in the United States. Many of the others also contribute to the hardship and exclusion that predispose persons to hate-based ideologies. Low wages, erratic schedules, few if any benefits, rising costs of living, all make distinct contributions to creating and incentivizing the familial and workplace experiences and conditions that facilitate the adoption of hate-based ideologies. The social consequences of low wages and precarious employment situations are no less significant.

Social exclusion and lack of opportunity, particularly in education, born from a lack of adequate economic resources, also forces many to attempt to rationalize the suffering that they experience. This mixture of exclusion and privation, leading to the need for explanation, combined with few economic or educational opportunities produces fertile ground for bringing individuals to hate-filled worldviews.

"Our system may have its problems, but they're not going to be solved by Nazism," assessed Joyce. "Eddie?" she queried directly.

"No comment, Joyce," he responded.

She realized she was putting a lot on his plate in front of his sister and mother but considering where he was coming from; she had to be hopeful of rescuing him – and herself. She couldn't resist mentioning, "The blatant use of the swastika on the emblem for the American Nazis Party is too much for many people."

"I can't abide it," contributed Millie.

"From what I know," it is a terrible symbol that celebrates evil," Audrey stated.

Are you aware of other Nazism organizations establishing themselves in the northwest, Eddie?" pursued Joyce. "Skinheads?"

"I have heard mention but I mostly just know about the Feistys," he responded. *And I don't know everything about them*, Eddie thought. *Just that I trust Frederic.*

"Do you want to check in with Frederic?" dared Joyce. "It's not even noon yet, and I won't be ready for sharing what's probably most important, until tomorrow." It was a white lie, well a lie but she wanted to give Eddie a breather before launching into the specific manifestations of violence in the Northwest, mostly Portland. "I can use Millie's and Audrey's help with my research," she further exaggerated.

Eddie arranged a lunch with Frederic and hoped it would be pleasant and fruitful. Frederic suggested Stammtisch German Restaurant at 401 NE 28th Ave, in Portland.

On arriving, Eddie looked for Frederic.

He was already there, and, as usual, greeted Eddie with a warm hug. He then invited Eddie to join him in a Pilsner beer. For lunch, Frederic recommended the sausage which they both ordered. Then Eddie decided to dive in for the first time and ask Frederic about himself.

"You know a lot about me, Frederic, but I don't know anything about you."

"What do you want to know?"

"Are you married, have any children?

"No and no," he chuckled. "What else?"

"Do you like women?"

"Of course, but there's no one I'm serious about, someone of the same thinking. The right person for me has to be, you know, also strong on White principles and

157

must, of course, be White. She'll come along, but until she does, I have plenty to do."

"Planning something big?"

"You are sharp, Eddie. Yes, something big. And you will be a part of it. Does that please you?"

There was only one answer to give. "Yes, Frederic."

"So, how does go with the **Jew**?" he asked.

"Under control," advised Eddie.

"Wonderful. I knew you were the right person for us. I am very excited about what's up ahead, but I can't tell you about it yet. Don't worry you're part of the team now, our **family,**" said Frederic**.**

Somehow it didn't quite go down right. *I know you'll tell me to kill Joyce,* he thought.

Frederic went on to expound over lunch some of the same things that Joyce was warning. What, who was he to believe? While he still had the chance, Eddie decided to press Frederic about his reasons for getting involved with the Feistys.

"Frederic, you have been very clear on Feistys values and intentions. Please share with me your personal attraction."

Frederic looked a bit taken back but replied, "Of course, Eddie. Like yourself, I had a miserable home life with a step-father who was a Jew bastard. I can't tell you how many times I wanted to smash in his hook-nosed Jewish face. Not a lot different than what you experienced. Feistys saved me just as they'll save you."

Eddie was not so sure, but lunch ended as did all of his meetings with Frederic – with a warm hug.

"Did you have a good get together," Joyce asked on his return. *Still going to kill me?* Joy wondered.

Chapter 13 – Violence I

Tues., Oct. 11, 2016, Home of Joyce Levinson, 9:00 AM

Eddie, Audrey, and Millie sat side by side in what had become their usual places on the sofa in the living room. They waited for Joyce, seated in the armchair, to begin.

Yesterday, Eddie thought, *Joyce said this was the day when she would be sharing what's probably most important.* She hadn't talked about it over breakfast, and Eddie decided not to press her on it.

Joyce broke the silence. "Okay, everything we've covered so far is, is, the preamble to what I will share next."

"Preamble?" questioned Audrey.

"Yes, *introduction*," explained Joyce. "Today we're going to go into, the actual activities of Neo-Nazi based organizations and people in the Northwest."

"Like Feistys?" asked Millie.

"Like Feistys but perhaps a little further along. Has Frederic mentioned anything about Feistys working on something, a plan?"

"No," lied Eddie.

Joyce suspected Eddie was holding back but decided not to pursue it. "I'm going to start with someone who does a lot to stir up trouble, although, to date, has not given himself over to an exertion of violence. Here's what the Anti-Defamation League said not long ago, on September 7, 2016." She gave out printouts and read:

Oregon Neo-Nazi Takes Anti-Semitic Message to the Highways

Jimmy Marr, a well-known neo-Nazi activist in Oregon, has taken to the highways to promote his anti-Semitic, white supremacist agenda. On July 17, 2016, Marr posted photographs on VNN Forum, a prominent neo-Nazi/ white supremacist social media site, showing off a truck, adorned signs reading "Jew Lies Matter" and "Truth Dispels Darkness," accompanied by a swastika. Marr recently began pairing this message with a "Blue Lives Matter" sign, because, as he explained in an August 2016 VNN post: "the Blue Lives/Jew Lies signage works well for me because it aligns my position with cops who might otherwise be unamused by my activism." In September, Marr re-painted the back of the truck

to read: "Trump: Do the White Thing."

"If this is what Trump needs to be elected and he is elected, we are in deep crap," observed Millie, "I will be working with Audrey to figure out someplace else to live in this world. Don't ask me where."

"Is NASA still sending space vehicles to the moon?" asked Audrey. "Want to come, Eddie? Oh, I forgot. You'd have to check in with Frederic first."

"Knock it off, little sister. You don't know anything about anything. Maybe Jimmy Marr is on the right track, and all we have to do is wait until he and others get things to a better place right here in Portland."

"Are you fully convinced of this, Eddie?" pressed Joyce. "Because if you are, we can quit this little charade right now and go our separate ways."

The conversation had gone much further than Eddie intended. He was still on the fence regarding Frederic and the Feistys and needed the information that Joyce was providing. "Please, Joyce," he implored, "this has gone way too far. When I said I wanted to know **everything,** I meant it, Jimmy Marr or no Jimmy Marr."

Joyce, Millie, and Audrey all breathed a sigh of relief. "Still proud of you," responded Joyce.

Millie and Audrey both nodded their agreement.

Joyce resumed reading.

This provocative joyriding is just the latest episode in Marr's long history of anti-Semitism and Neo-Nazi activism. Best known for sporting a kilt and playing bagpipes while leading racist and anti-Semitic protests around Oregon and the U.S., Marr has been an active Neo-Nazi since 2009. He first made news when Oregon recalled his personal license plate, which read, "NO ZOG," a reference to the "Zionist Occupied Government," an anti-Semitic conspiracy theory that claims the U.S. and other world governments are controlled by a Jewish/Israeli cabal.

Further notoriety came his way when he was a featured speaker at The Pacifica Forum, an independent group in Eugene formed by a retired professor at the University of Oregon (not affiliated with the university), which regularly sponsored lectures by anti-Semites and Holocaust deniers. In 2009, Marr gave a presentation to the group entitled "The National Socialist Movement: An Inside View of America's Far-Right." During the meeting, according to a member of Eugene's Anti-Hate Task Force, Marr expressed the view white DNA is not being sufficiently protected. A year earlier, speaking at the same forum, Marr reportedly called Martin Luther King, Jr., a "moral leper, and Communist dupe," and gave a Nazi salute.

In 2011 and 2012, Marr marched with the National Socialist Movement in Nevada and California, and in 2012, Marr posted the following on the anti-Semitic Zion Crime Factory website: "I embarked on a regimen of one man street demonstrations last month in which I did

street performances on the bagpipes while wearing a sign that read 'Anti-racism is a code word for anti-White.'" In 2013, he was one of the several white supremacists who attempted to take control of the City of Leith, North Dakota, to create a home for whites. (Their doomed efforts were immortalized in the 2015 documentary film "Welcome to Leith").

When Marr takes to the internet, his postings are, unsurprisingly, very anti-Semitic. In a 2012 Facebook post, he wrote: "There once lived a people, far beyond hope whose daughters were whores. Sons on dope with a conscious decision, they watched Talmudvision, let their brains be washed with Jewish soap."

"What a nice guy!" Joyce commented.

"He didn't personally do anything," attempted Eddie.

"Yes, just stirred up as much crap as possible to get others to do the dirty work. Let's move on," Joyce said. She handed out another printout from which she was about to read.

"May I," offered Millie.

"My pleasure," Joyce happily replied.

Audrey patted her mother on the back, and Millie began.

From Tyler Dunn, KOIN Web Staff, Published: July 18, 2014, 10:00 am Updated: July 19, 2014, 10:35 pm

Exposed: The Northwest's white supremacy problem James Sapp example of OR, WA white supremacist violence.

"Note, " pointed out Joyce, "that KOIN Tyler Dunn identifies James Sapp as an **example** of OR, WA white supremacist violence. An EXAMPLE!"

Eddie could not miss Joy's upset. *She's afraid of the Feistys and what I might do.* "We get it, Joyce. Please go easy on yourself. Continue reading, Ma."

Joyce sat back in her chair and nodded her agreement.

James Todd Sapp, accused of shooting Vancouver Officer Dustin Goudschall during a traffic stop, made his first court appearance on July 1, 2014 (KOIN 6 News)

VANCOUVER, Wash. (KOIN 6) — A hail of gunfire, an officer down.

Shot seven times, Vancouver police officer Dustin Goudschaal lay on the street struggling for his life as a passerby did her best to bandage a gunshot wound to the 32-year-old's neck.

"Shot seven times," muttered Audrey while shaking her head.

Only moments earlier, Goudschaal had stopped a Dodge pickup that was flagged for a stolen license plate. Goudschaal wasn't even at the truck's driver door when a man arched a black semi-automatic handgun out the window and fired.

Investigators say James Sapp shot a police officer and a passenger, assaulted several others and crashed two stolen vehicles in less than 20 minutes.

"Perhaps, he was influenced by Jimmy Marr," Joyce suggested.

"We don't know that," responded Eddie.

"Well, something got to him, and the result is ugly," Joyce insisted, "and nearby here right in the Northwest, recently. You dig in and read some," she instructed Eddie, somewhat irritated. "Okay, Millie?"

Eddie's mother nodded, and he began.

The shooting was only the beginning of the violence that took place on Vancouver's streets June 30. James Sapp — now identified as the Dodge driver and charged with Goudschaal's attempted murder — admittedly drove away after the officer fell to the ground.

Sapp, 48, crashed the truck into a tree four blocks away. Probable cause court records, documenting testimony from multiple witnesses and victims, depict Sapp's next movements as a frenzied, ever-escalating getaway attempt, though his retelling often places him outside any blame.

According to the affidavit, Sapp shot at his passenger, punched a woman twice in the face in an attempt to steal her car, assaulted an 88-year-old man in another carjacking attempt, and hurt two others as he sped away.

Minutes later, Sapp had crashed that vehicle as well. By 11:55 a.m. — just 17 minutes after the first 911 officer-shot call was placed — Sapp was found "hiding behind metal dumpsters."

SEE THE DOCUMENTS

More than a gram of heroin, 3.5 grams of methamphetamine and 38.7 grams of marijuana were also found near the dumpster and in Sapp's pocket, court documents state.

Who is James Sapp?

Sapp appeared in court three times since that day, the latest being Tuesday when he entered a not guilty plea for the Goudschaal shooting and the later-added drug charges.

Known as "Cotton" on the streets, Sapp admits he's been a heroin user for the past six years, documents state. With a shaved, balding head and scraggly beard, the heavily tattooed, 230-pound Sapp is an intimidating presence.

*But it's the group he claims to be affiliated with that's most troubling. Sapp, who has a large tattoo of a swastika and the words "White Pride" inked across his lower back, told a Clark County jail deputy in 2008 "he is a member of the Aryan Brotherhood" and that "he would not **be housed** with anyone of color."*

"Naturally," Audrey emphasized.

Three years earlier, Sapp allegedly told Gresham police "he is an active member of the Aryan Brotherhood" and that he "kept in touch with his brothers behind bars."

According to Southern Poverty Law Center, a hate group watchdog, "Aryan Brotherhood members make up less than one-tenth of one percent of the nation's prison inmate population, yet the white power gang is responsible for 18% of all prison murders."

Former member: Aryan Brotherhood all about crime

Only one other man involved in white supremacist activity in the Portland area has been linked to the AB in recent years, according to Multnomah County Sheriff's Office officials. That man — 35-year-old Justin Dodson

— killed himself last June when law enforcement tried to arrest him on drug and gun charges.

A three-leaf clover tattoo consistently seen among members of the Aryan Brotherhood. James Sapp has no known tattoo. (policemag.com)

Whether Sapp is an actual member of the infamous white supremacist organization is up for debate, but Randy Blazak, a Portland State University sociology professor, says his alleged actions are in line with the gang's tactics.

"There's this thing called 'doing the dirt' while you're in prison. You're protected by the Brotherhood, but for that, you have to pay the price," Blazak said in an attempt to explain a possible motive. "It's called 'credit.' Sometimes that price is paid inside, but sometimes it's paid outside. You have to kill somebody."

Far From Just the Brotherhood

Even if Sapp has no affiliation with the AB, he still may well be an active gang member.

Blazak says lesser-known white supremacist gangs are on the rise across the Pacific Northwest.

"Across the Pacific Northwest!" Joyce repeated. "Do you all see where we've come?"

"Calm yourself, Joyce," a concerned Eddie responded. "Maybe we should stop."

Joyce shook her head, took a minute and seemed to settle herself. "Please continue reading, Eddie," she started when Audrey put up her hand.

"I can read," the young woman offered.

There were no objections, and Joyce nodded to her, to begin with where they left off with Blazak.

Chapter 14 – Violence II

Audrey began with where they left off with Blazak.

"It's a growing issue ... Tthe notion that whites have the numbers," he said. "They think it's the white bastion."

Blazak even points out a movement that gained steam in the 1980s among white nationalists called the "Northwest Territorial Imperative." Under the concept, Idaho, Oregon, Washington, and the western part of Montana would form a new colony known as the "White Homeland."

The SPLC supports the professor's claim, listing nine hate groups in Oregon and ten in Washington, of which the large majority are classified as "Racist Skinhead," "White Nationalist," or "Neo-Nazi."

"Nine hate groups in Oregon and ten in Washington!" exclaimed Millie. "We must have our heads buried in the sand to be so oblivious to this. Aren't we making it way too easy for these hate mongers to exist and do whatever they want?"

"I think so," put in Joyce.

"Me too," agreed Audrey.

There was a part of him that also wanted to agree, but Eddie was not ready to give up on Frederic and the Feistys. He shrugged once again.

Joyce nodded to Audrey to continue reading.

Operation White Christmas

The gangs have shown a proclivity to pop up around the Portland metro, and in the past year, the Multnomah County Sheriff's Office has come down hard on them.

Operation White Christmas, as the now-high-profile effort was dubbed, began last summer and had netted some substantial arrests.

"The overall success has been huge," said Josh Zwick, MCSO's lead case detective for the crackdown. "We got some very nasty people off the streets."

MCSO officials say the operation came about after "a huge amount of violent crime" in and around East Portland.

Since OWC's first bust, more than 80 people that investigators say are tied to white supremacist gangs have been arrested, 48 of whom are currently undergoing federal prosecution, according to Zwick.

Twenty-seven OWC-related warrants have been served in that time, Zwick says. Among the items seized: more than nine pounds of methamphetamine; 90 guns; 50 grams of heroin; $78,000; three bulletproof vests; a stolen RV; four vehicles; a violin and other high-end musical instruments; credit cards; social security cards; driver's license templates; motorcycle parts and about 30 rare coins stolen from Oregon State University's Horner Collection.

Multiple explosives were also recovered and then disposed of.

Most of the arrests are connected to a handful of gangs in the Portland area: the European Kindred (EK); Rude Krude Brood; Irish Pride; All Ona Bitch (ONA); Insane Peckerwood Syndicate (IPS) and Fat Bitch Killers (FBK).

Eddie was relieved the list didn't include the Feistys, and Joyce decided to relieve Audrey of the reading.

"You've done well, Audrey," praised Joyce. "You can pick up again in a bit today or tomorrow. Okay?"

"Yes, Joyce. Thank you," replied Audrey

Joyce once again began reading.

Zwick says White Christmas has almost entirely dismantled the gangs' primary leadership in Multnomah County but stops short of saying the operation is complete. Every time we think it's over, it's not, he says.

'A Racism of Convenience'

Zwick and Blazak agree these gangs are about more than racial hatred — it's a business fostered from fear and one that starts in prison.

As Blazak explains it, gangs like EK, the Brood, and ONA are formed in prisons across the region as a form of protection, something he calls "a racism of convenience."

"Racism's a weapon, a tool," said Blazak, who further suggested many white supremacist gang members are actually of mixed ancestry.

But what starts as an act of survival quickly shifts to a life of crime once released, Blazak says. "It looks more like organized crime than the KKK," he said.

And once in a supremacist gang, getting out is not an easy feat.

These guys come out of prison as convicted felons with swastika tattoos, Zwick said. "They're not friendly people. [Being a gang member] is all they know, that's what they keep doing."

Down the Rabbit Hole

Blazak blames the rise in white supremacist crime on poor prison policy dating back two decades. The "War on Drugs," pursued heavily in the 1980s and 1990s, inflated incarceration rates and led to the creation of many of the gangs causing issues for law enforcement today, Blazak says.

And while white supremacist gangs are far from the only perpetrators of violent crime in Multnomah County — County officials recently released a report identifying 133 known gangs active in the area — the sociology professor doesn't think white supremacists attempting to re-enter society have been given the proper resources.

Lt. Steve Alexander, the spokesman for the Multnomah County Sheriff's Office, says he recognizes a cycle of violence and imprisonment as well but says prisoners are given every opportunity to leave their past behind.

According to Alexander, the goal is to weaken gangs "from the inside."

"Well," Millie remarked, "with 133 known gangs, their efforts are not very impressive."

"Unbelievable," added Audrey.

Eddie once again shrugged.

Trying to send a message to Eddie, Joyce responded, "I'm glad to have the balance you both provide, Millie, and Audrey. Eddie, please pick up on the reading."

Sapp's history with law enforcement indicates he's more than familiar with the cycle. Having been convicted of drugs charges four times and once more for riot with a deadly weapon, Sapp now faces his most daunting allegations yet.

Thursday, the Clark County Sheriff's Office announced Sapp had tried to kill himself from his jail cell. Deputies were said to have intervened and rushed him to a local hospital, but medical personnel were unable to save him. He was pronounced dead at 12:45 p.m. Friday.

Wed., Oct. 12, 2016, Home of Joyce Levinson, 8:00 AM

They were all still shook up by the revelations of the prior day and ate breakfast in silence. Eddie at last, asked, "Can we stop now?"

"There are three more incidents," advised Joyce, "that I've come across of which I feel we should review. Then, Eddie, you can add it all up regarding Feistys and your life." *My life too*, she thought.

Millie and Audrey were thunderstruck by the obvious significance of what was happening. They decided to remain silent.

The four of them subsequently moved to the living room, where Joyce proceeded with reading after distributing printouts about the next incident.

Man with Nazi tattoos in custody for 3 Woodland murders

Three people found dead at one house, another wounded woman found elsewhere.

KOIN 6 News Staff
Published: July 16, 2016, 5:51 am. Updated: July 16, 2016, 8 pm

"Talk about decorating yourself," commented Joyce. "Does doing something like that turn anybody here on? Eddie?" She asked.

"No way, Joy," he responded. "You, Ma, Audrey?"

"Never when I was younger, and I'm not about to decorate what's left of me at 61," confided Joyce.

"Me too, " put in Millie.

"And me," added Audrey.

Finally, realized Eddie, they were all together on something.

"Want to read for a while, Eddie?" Joyce asked.

"Sure," he answered without a pause, in spite of his nervousness about the three murders.

WOODLAND, Wash. (KOIN) — A man with numerous Nazi tattoos is the prime suspect in a triple murder that happened late Friday in Woodland.

A Confederate flag hangs over the house where police say Brent Luyster killed three people. (KOIN)

Brent W. Luyster, 35, was taken into custody without incident by Cowlitz County Deputies as Washington State Troopers at 4:15 p.m. Saturday. He was in a Gold Ford Explorer on Ocean Beach Hwy.

Woodland police officers found a woman shot in the face around 10:20 p.m. Friday at the AM/PM store on CC Street. They learned a shooting happened at 4006 NW 417th Street and brought in the Clark County Sheriff's Office and Southwest Regional SWAT unit.

Three people were found dead at that location. None of the victims has been identified publicly at this time.

He was considered armed and extremely dangerous.

The Clark County Major Crimes Unit will continue its investigation.

Previous arrests

In May, Luyster allegedly pistol whipped his 32-year-old ex-girlfriend, who is the mother of his child.

When police responded to arrest Luyster at his house, they heard gunfire from the woods nearby. Deputies thought he was shooting at them and eventually talked him into surrendering.

He was charged with 2nd-degree assault, nine counts of unlawful possession of firearms and reckless endangerment.

In 2013, Luyster, his brother Robert and a man named Donald McElfish were arrested for an alleged racial attack at the QuarterDeck Bar in Vancouver.

All three have ties to a white supremacy group and were charged with that time with 2nd-degree felony assault and racially-motivated malicious harassment incident.

The men arrived at the tavern, saw a black man sitting with a white woman at the bar. Court documents at that time said Brent Luyster made a racially pointed remark about it. Robert Luyster shouted a threat, got a gun from his car, put a bullet into the chamber, stepped outside and pointed the gun at three people standing there.

Robert then gave the gun to his brother Brent, who also began to threaten the three men. The Luysters left in McElfish's car when they heard the police coming.

The Luyster's court documents said, hold racist beliefs and have previously been associated with the Skinheads.

"Well that was uplifting," shared Joyce in a contrary manner. How is everyone doing with all this?"

"Frightening," said Millie.

"Terrible," answered Audrey.

Eddie surprisingly responded, "It's awful, Joyce. How much do you have left?"

Millie and Audrey suddenly realized this was a more extraordinary situation than was obvious to them.

"Two more Oregon events that you shouldn't miss, Eddie," Joyce advised. Then I'll feel that I've given you the grounding to make your decision on how you want to live out the rest of your life. "It'll be 'The Lady or The Tiger.' Ever hear of that?"

"No, Joyce."

Audrey and Millie looked at one another and smiled knowingly.

"Well, that'll be a lesson for another day," Joyce replied. For now, you just need to know that I'm the lady and that leaves Frederic and the Feistys the role of..."

"The tiger," Eddie finished.

"Okay, my friend, we're coming down the 'pike.' I'll read the next account and leave the last one for you."

The anti-Christ shooter is a teetotaling Nazi

By Joe Tacopino, October 1, 2015, | 11:54 pm

White Supremacy

Chris Harper-Mercer, the gunman who went on Thursday's rampage at an Oregon college, idolized the Nazis and the IRA, despised organized religion — and talked about how killing could bring a person fame.

"What a discovery," observed Audrey, "the road to fame!"

"This is one twisted individual," commented Millie.

"What to **you** think, Eddie," asked Joyce.

"Needs focus," responded Eddie.

"Fiesty focus?" pursued Joyce.

"Maybe," Eddie answered.

Joyce decided not to respond and continued reading.

"I have noticed that so many people like [Vester Lee Flanagan] are alone and unknown, yet when they spill a little blood, the whole world knows who they are," Harper-Mercer wrote in a blog post, referring to the man who in August murdered a reporter and a cameraman on live TV in Virginia, <u>according to CBS News.</u>

"A man who was known by no one is now known by everyone. His face splashed across every screen, his name across the lips of every person on the planet, all in the course of one day. Seems like the more people you kill, the more you're in the limelight."

He also showed interest in the Virginia Tech and Sandy Hook school shootings, recently having shared documentaries about the massacres with people online.

Allen Pollens

Chapter 15 – Violence III

A profile on an online dating site, Spiritual Passions, shows the 26-year-old Harper-Mercer "doesn't like organized religion" and identified as a "conservative Republican."

Joyce, a longtime Democrat, said, "Republicans can have him."

"I don't think they'd want him any more than the Democrats," Eddie responded.

They all chuckled, and Joy went on reading.

On his MySpace page, he posted some pictures related to the Irish Republican Army.

"He appears to be an angry young man who was very filled with hate," one source told The New York Times.

A man who answered the phone at the home of a relative of Harper-Mercer told The Post the young man lived earlier in California's LA County but moved out of state.

At a press conference about the shootings at Umpqua Community College late Thursday, Douglas County Sheriff John Hanlin refused to utter the shooter's name, said the focus should be on victims and their families.

Harper-Mercer, who lived in Winchester, OR. identified himself as mixed race. On the dating site, he wrote he does not smoke or drink.

His name on the site was Ironcross45, alluding to a Nazi military badge.

He also used the moniker on the website to laud the excellent "customer service" received when ordering a leather Nazi SS officer's cap.

"I have received my order," the user wrote. "The customer service is the very best; they are fast and very great to work with. I highly recommend this company they are a great pleasure to work with. their attention to detail is awesome."

In another blog post, Harper-Mercer mentioned the murders of NYPD Officers Wenjian Liu and Rafael Ramos, saying the Black Lives Matter group may have been to blame.

"With the constant chants of anti-police rhetoric this was bound to happen," he wrote. "Killing an officer that didn't do anything to you is not the answer."

"Okay, Eddie, you're on with the final recent incident," Joy urged.

Eddie began reading.

White Supremacists Cheer on Oregon Neo-Nazi Who Ran Over Black Teen

September 2, 2016, <u>Racism</u>

A black teenager in a Portland, Oregon, suburb was killed by a white supremacist gang member in what police say was an intentional hit-and-run.

Larnell Bruce, 19, had just recently moved to Gresham to live with family when he encountered a notoriously violent neo-Nazi named Russell Courtier outside of a 7-Eleven on August 10. 38-year-old Courtier spent time in prison, where he belonged to the European Kindred—a white supremacist gang, founded in Malheur County, a few miles from where a conservative white militia staged an armed takeover of a wildlife refuge in January.

As the Portland Mercury reported Wednesday, a fight broke out between the gang member and the teen—with Courtier smashing Bruce's head into the glass storefront of the 7-Eleven. The clerk called the police, and Bruce ran. Courtier and girlfriend, 35-year-old Colleen Hunt, got in their Jeep and chased Bruce across sidewalks and oncoming traffic in the vehicle. Finally, they mowed him down, leaving the police to find the teen "in the middle of the street with blood rushing from his head and ears."

Bruce died in the hospital a few days after police found him mangled by the hit-and-run.

After Courtier was arrested for the murder, the Mercury reported that several local white supremacists and members of the European Kindred (EK) gang were posting messages of support for Courtier on Facebook.

"They tested kindred and homeboy did not hesitate," wrote one alleged EK member.

Screengrab via Portland Mercury

The Mercury revealed that Courtier had a long and violent record of which law enforcement authorities were fully aware. At the time he killed Bruce, Courtier was still on parole for attacking a woman with a knife. His record includes seven felony and four misdemeanor convictions, over 40 prison violations during time served, and a series of incidents in which Courtier was given probation or dropped charges—even after police found him shooting a gun out of his car window in 2011, or bashing his fiancé's head into a car windshield in 2012.

On Thursday, after the New York Daily News, ' Shaun King wrote about the killing, black Twitter users and anti-racism advocates posted distressed and saddened messages. Many of the tweets compared the lack of media attention on the murder to the exorbitant amount of press devoted to NFL quarterback Colin Kaepernick's decision to sit during national anthems at games—a quiet protest that has caused angry fans to burn their 49ers jerseys.

Eddie looked one last time at the picture of the teen before laying down the printout. He could not hold back the avalanche of tears for Bruce and all of the others whose lives were taken. He raised himself from the sofa to find Joyce, Millie, and Audrey standing and also crying. They held one another for a long time.

Then Eddie pleaded, "What am I going to do?"
"Don't worry," offered Joyce. "You've come a long way and tomorrow's another day. I'm proud of you."
"We all are," Millie and Audre voiced together.

Thursday, Oct. 13, 2016, Joyce's Home, 8:00 AM

Eddie awoke in a new frame of mind. Joyce showed him the horrors of Nazism, and his mother and sister helped him know it was true. He could only be against someone if they posed a danger. He knew he had to be strong to protect himself, Joyce, his mother, and his sister

When Eddie came into the kitchen for breakfast, the others immediately sensed an important change in him. He stood taller and conveyed an air of confidence.

"Good morning, Eddie," Joyce greeted. "We've been waiting for you. Breakfast is ready. Have a seat."

Eddie went to his recently usual seating between Millie and Audrey. However, he initially stood behind the chair with his hands resting on the top of the back.

"I am a new man today," he declared, "a person open to helping anyone in need, regardless of religious belief, ancestry, or skin color. If it would not get in the way, I'd like to have two mothers, just one sister. Ma, you would be my Hillsboro mother, and Joyce my Portland mother if she would like me to be the son you never had. Ma?"

"What a lovely idea," Millie expressed. "I love it, and I love you, Eddie."

Joyce, with tears in her eyes, got up and went to where Eddie stood. She kissed him on the cheek and said, "I love you, my son."

"As do I," said Millie. She too kissed his cheek.

"Don't leave me out," insisted Audrey who also kissed him on the cheek.

Eddie waited until the three returned to their seats and then advised, "I will do my best to protect you all from harm. I would like to go back to school and learn to be a writer. My first article would advise that people need to be giving but guarded against those, increasingly among us, who would inflict pain and even kill us."

"Those are wonderful goals, Eddie. I am with you 100%," Joyce said.

Millie and Audrey in unison said, "We all are."

Joyce then declared, "This is a day beyond my fondest dreams, a day to celebrate. Let's all dance down the street and into the city."

The walked the streets and especially enjoyed the downtown parks. Some people joined in and followed them for some distance. Before they knew it, they were gazing, across Burnside, at the entrance to Chinatown.

They walked down the street looking for a place to eat. On the way, Eddie told everyone they encountered, "It's celebration day, it's celebration day."

Joyce added, "Celebrate this wonderful gift of life." Millie contributed, "Don't let creeps put you down." Audrey shouted out, "Live the Day."

Passersby were a little puzzled, but most gave into the spirit of the moment. Some shouted, "Hooray!"

They picked Chan's, a street level restaurant. The ambiance and food were great. Eddie was high on his new-found freedom and promises of opportunities ahead. Joyce, Millie, and Audrey enjoyed his happiness. Joyce was especially ecstatic in the realization of what she and Eddie had come through. She thought of something else to do. "Follow me," she ordered as they exited Chan's.

A few blocks away, Eddie, Millie, and Audrey waited while Joyce bought tickets at the entrance to the

Chinese Garden. Then, they stepped into a beautiful new world such as they had never before experienced.

All of Eddie's fears of the Feistys and the steadily increasing Nazism in Portland momentarily vanished. Joyce observed his current child-like enjoyment of the moment and did her best to encourage it. *The outside world will not so easily let go of us, Eddie,* she thought, *so make the most of the day and enjoy 'living the daylights' out of it.*

They returned home by late afternoon, and Eddie broke the spell when alone with Joyce, he advised, "I need my gun."

"What?!" she exclaimed.

"Calm down, please," Eddie requested. "Only for a little while, until I'm sure we are all safe from Frederic and the Feistys. Then, I'll either drop it in the Willamette or turn it over to the police."

"Are you seriously worried about Frederic and the Feistys?" Joyce wanted to know.

"No," Eddie lied, "and I'll deal with it. Still, until I know, we are all safe, I need my gun."

Joyce had her reservations but, in the end, returned the gun.

Several days went by, and everything seemed *cool.* Then Eddie received a call from Frederic. "It's time, Eddie. Come down to the office, **now!**"

Chapter 16 – Feistys

Eddie made up an excuse and somehow managed to get himself over to the Feistys office.

There were four other men with Frederic. They looked about the same age as Eddie, or perhaps a little older.

"Welcome, Eddie," Frederic greeted. "Hey everyone," he continued, "Here's Eddie."

Eddie was soon fully engulfed by the other Feistys. They wanted to know all about him and readily shared their stories as well. Just when he thought he was never going to get free of them, Frederic broke in and begged their indulgence while he had a few minutes alone with Eddie. Frederic ushered Eddie into another room that was immediately connected. It looked to be set up originally as an outer greeting area for the larger room from which they had come. It was clearly not currently in use and dimly lit.

Frederic motioned for Eddie to make use of a desk side chair even as he backed to and sat partially on the desk.

"This is it," Frederic happily disclosed. "The plan is set and will take place at River Front Park. I'm looking forward to your full participation, but you'll have to dispose of Levinson, first."

"Frederic," Eddie responded, "that's not going to happen."

Frederic paused, clearly a taken back. He reached over and pinched Eddie's shoulder while angrily informing, "It's going to take place with or without you, but better with you."

Eddie pulled away from the painful pinch and stood up. "I don't want to be a Fiesty and hurt anyone."

"What? How dare you!" Frederic screamed out.

I'm leaving," Eddie said even as he raced into the main room, pushed Frederic's underlings aside and dashed out the door.

Joyce was alone in the living room when Eddie returned to the house. She knew immediately from the look on his face that something was very wrong. "What happened, Eddie?" Joyce pressed.

He told her, and her first reaction was, "I'm going to call the police."

"He'll deny it, Joyce," he responded. "It'll be my word against his."

"But you said you know they are coming, just not when, Eddie."

"Yes, but I have my gun, and right now we need to lock all windows and doors and drop the shades. We can order in food as needed."

Eddie and Joyce found Millie and Audrey sitting at the kitchen table and talking.

"How brave are you?" Joyce asked them.

Then Eddie told them everything.

"They're not taking us alive," Audrey quoted a famous Clint Eastwood line.

"Yes," Millie said shaking her head, "but let's create a surprise for Frederic and company. Eddie has a gun. What else do we have available we can use as weapons?"

"Kitchen carving knives and some long handled pots and pans," volunteered Joyce. "Also, there are, garden tools, a shovel, metal rake and more in the basement."

"Rope?" questioned Eddie.

"That too, is in the basement," replied Joyce.

Before long they were ready. It was just a matter of waiting. Each had an agreed upon station based on the belief Frederic would not be alone. They expected Frederic and the other four Feistys, Eddie had seen in the Feistys office.

Eddie guarded the front door. He didn't like the idea of it but felt the gun had to be his primary weapon. He'd never shot anyone. *Maybe I won't have to use it today,* he wished. Yet he knew he had to be strong and not hesitate to use the gun if necessary.

Millie and Audry were nearby each gaurding one of the ground level front double hung windows of which there were exactly two. They wished they had real weapons. They were nevertheless determined to use the garden tools they found in the basement to the fullest. They breathed heavily in the quiet and periodically checked with Eddie to make sure he was okay and prepared.

Joyce was alone guarding the second floor door leading to the open porch. Anyone seeking entry there would first have to climb up onto the porch. It was unfortunately not difficult to do. Further, she only had what she had found in the kitchen to use as weapons.

The waiting was difficult, but then, near 7:30 PM the Feistys attacked everywhere. Two tried to come in through ground floor windows.

Millie and Audrey stood ready. They watched and waited until a head showed itself through each of two windows.

"Now!" shouted Millie as she brought the spade shovel down as hard as possible, knocking the first entrant out.

"Yeow!" screamed Audrey as she as well brought down a landscape rake with its multiple short metal fingers driving down onto the second intruder.

With their stations fully under control, Millie, as instructed, used her cell phone to call the police.

Joyce, standing on a chair and guarding the upper-level porch door,

used heavy long-handled fry pans, one in each hand, to clobber the third invader. She also called the police who said they were already underway.

Eddie was ready at the front door,

when Frederic kicked it open. He raised and pointed his gun at Eddie when, ***BOOM,*** Eddie put a bullet into Frederic's right eye.

Frederic fell to the floor. Eddie thought it was, at last, all over when he heard another shot and felt a sharp pain in his chest.

Frederic's underling in training did what he was supposed to do and seemed confused as the arriving police took him into custody.

Joyce, Millie, and Audrey watched, horrified, as the ambulance placed an unconscious Eddie on a gurney and wheeled him to the medical vehicle.

The bullet passed close to Eddie's heart, and he lost a lot of blood. Several days went by with Joyce, Millie, and Audrey sharing in a 24-hr vigil.

The hospital staff was extremely helpful. However, they periodically reminded them that Eddie might not make it. Joyce especially consistently replied through her tears, "He will make it!"

When Eddie finally awakened, he looked around the room and realized he was in the hospital. He was connected to several pieces o monitoring equipment, including some of which were beeping or making other sounds. Then he saw Joyce, sitting next the bed holding his hand and asleep. "Hi sleepyhead," he ventured.

Joyce shook herself awake and jumped up out of her chair when she realized Eddie had awakened. Then she ran out into the hallway to get the doctors and nurses, and to find Millie and Audrey. She found them in the cafeteria and rushed them back to Eddie's room. Nurses told them when they got there they would have to stay in the waiting room until the doctors finished their examination.

About thirty minutes later they finished examining Eddie and declared him on the way to a full recovery. A very tired Joyce slumped back down in her chair next to the bed and delivered a broad happy smile to Eddie. On each side of her sat exhausted Millie and Audrey.

After a few minutes, Eddie asked, "What happened?"

"You shot Frederic," informed Joyce, "and saved us, me, your mother and your sister. Frederic is dead, and the police are holding the other Feistys in custody, charged with attempted murder."

"Now, what? " asked Eddie.

"Now, we have to work on getting you well, and we all have a lot to do," advised Joyce.

Eddie could only guess at what all was up ahead. He loved his Ma and sister but knew especially that with Joyce, it would all be a Joy.

Epilogue

With Frederic and the Feistys out of the way, Joyce and Eddie did their best to lead happy, productive lives. They thoroughly enjoyed the participation of Eddie's Ma and sister. However, they were careful to avoid the seemingly ever present Neo-Nazi organizations and their members. They did their best to work with law enforcement people and groups seeking to eliminate this Northwest disease. They were happiest when they could help a young person find a better way.

For kind, Joyce, this was an unexpected gift. Her pleasure increased as Eddie brought a wife and grandchildren into her life. However, in the dark of the night, she would often gaze out the window of the darkened room to make sure there were no hate-demons on the street. She knew they could move someplace else but was unwilling to leave the city she loved, Portland. Besides, was any place safe anymore?

21306377R00120

Printed in Great Britain
by Amazon